EMBRACING GRACE:

FINDING GOD IN EVERYDAY MOMENTS

CALYN BALDWIN

Editor: Maria Gracia Olorga, PhD
All Scripture quotations, unless otherwise noted, are taken from Bible Gateway: New International Version (NIV)

Table of Contents

DEDICATION

For my husband, Sean, my safe place, my greatest love and constant source of strength. Your unwavering belief in me, even when I doubted myself, is the reason I had the courage to write this book.

For my precious daughter, Calee, my heart outside my body and my greatest inspiration. This book is a piece of me, but my greatest story will always be you.

For my mom, Lenia, the woman who taught me resilience, kindness, and the power of unconditional love. Every word I write carries a piece of you because you are the reason I found my voice.

For my dad, Carlos Sr., who is everywhere in my heart and memories. Your love still carries me forward.

For my amazing brothers, Carlos Jr., Cannon, Calvin, and Caliv, my lifelong friends and protectors, you always remind me that family is forever.

And for my wonderful in-laws, Linda and Porter, for embracing me as one of your own, for your love and support that have meant more than I could ever express.

This book reflects the love, strength, and support you have all given me. With all my love and gratitude, this is for you.

ABOUT THE AUTHOR

Calyn Baldwin, MA.Ed has dedicated her life to guiding others on their spiritual journeys. With a strong academic background in Psychology and Religious Education, she brings a unique blend of professional insights and heartfelt reflections to her writing.

Her extensive experience as a Campus Minister and Retreats and Recollections Facilitator at De La Salle University Dasmariñas in the Philippines has profoundly shaped her approach to faith and spirituality. Through her active participation in youth ministry and faith formation programs, she has touched the lives of many, fostering spiritual growth and meaningful connections within the campus community.

Driven by her commitment to these principles, she has crafted this book that invites readers to embark on their own journeys of faith and discovery. Her personal stories, enriched with timeless biblical truths, offer comfort, guidance, and inspiration to those seeking a deeper connection with God.

The author shares her faith experiences with the hope of inspiring others to grow closer to God and deepen their spiritual paths. Her genuine passion for faith and her dedication to helping others shine through in every chapter, making this book a valuable companion for anyone on a spiritual journey.

A GRATEFUL HEART

"Give thanks in all circumstances, for this is God's will for you in Christ Jesus."

(1 Thessalonians 5:18)

Growing up, my parents instilled in my brothers and me the importance of gratitude. They taught us to appreciate every blessing, no matter how small. Family dinners were special, with each of us sharing something we were grateful for that day. These moments planted deep seeds of gratitude within me. Reflecting on my life now, I see countless reasons to give thanks.

I'm grateful for my life itself—the simple joy of waking up each morning fills me with appreciation. The unconditional love and support of my parents, who sacrificed so much for our well-being, have been a cornerstone in my life. Their unwavering belief in me gave me the courage to pursue my dreams. The laughter shared with my brothers, the inside jokes and childhood memories have created bonds that time and distance cannot weaken.

My husband, my partner, and my anchor supports my ambitions and shares in my joys and challenges. His love is a guiding light, especially in tough times. My heart swells with gratitude for my daughter, a precious gift who brings immense joy into our lives. Every giggle and milestone reminds me of the beauty of life and the deep love within our family.

I also cherish my in-laws and friends, who enrich my journey in ways words cannot express. Their presence reminds me of the importance of community. Each of these relationships is a thread in the tapestry of my life, creating a beautiful pattern of love and support.

Reflecting on my experiences—both painful and joyous—I realize they've all shaped me into the woman I am today, and for that, I am deeply thankful. My gifts and talents, strengths and weaknesses all contribute to my unique individuality and resilience.

One of the most beautiful expressions of communal gratitude is our church fellowship gatherings. I remember the warmth and generosity that radiated from everyone the first time I attended one. Seeing our church family come together to share food and stories filled my heart with joy. These gatherings are a powerful reminder of the generosity that flows from hearts full of thanks.

Each gathering is more than just a meal; it's a celebration of the blessings we each receive. In those moments, I feel the beauty of shared gratitude. Each dish brought to the table reflects love and effort, symbolizing our collective gratitude. We are all intertwined in this journey of faith. These gatherings are sacred times where we share our lives and grow in faith together. In these moments of communal gratitude, I see God's love most clearly, and I am reminded of the importance of fellowship and the beauty of a thankful heart. Each encounter reinforces the idea that shared gratitude transforms isolated moments into collective joy.

Dear God,

I praise and thank You for all the blessings You have bestowed upon me and my loved ones. Each day, Your grace and love shower us with countless gifts, both seen and unseen. Forgive me for the moments of ungratefulness when pride and self-centeredness cloud my heart. Help me to remember that without You, I am nothing, and everything I have is because of Your boundless generosity.

Lord, let me never forget that all I possess and all I am is a reflection of Your love and mercy. Do not allow pride to blind me or lead me away from You. Grant me a grateful heart that constantly acknowledges Your goodness and gives thanks for every blessing, every trial, and every moment. May I live each day in humble gratitude, recognizing Your hand in all things.

Thank You, Lord, for everything You have done and continue to do in my life. Your faithfulness is my strength, and Your love is my guide. I humbly offer my thanks and praise, trusting in Your eternal goodness.

Amen.

A Journey Back to God's Embrace

"Call to me and I will answer you and tell you great and unsearchable things you do not know."

(Jeremiah 33:3)

There was a time when I felt myself drifting away from God. I stopped talking to Him and barely noticed His presence in my life. It was as if I had shut the door on a relationship that once filled me with so much joy and comfort. Life's challenges and frustrations engulfed me, and I found myself feeling exhausted and disconnected.

In those tough times, it felt like I was stuck at the bottom of a deep pit. I wanted out, but somehow, I convinced myself that keeping my distance from God was my best option. I really believed I could manage everything on my own and navigate my struggles without His guidance. But as my heart weighed heavier, I came to realize how much I yearned for His love and support, even while I resisted it.

Yet God didn't leave me to struggle alone. He brought people into my life who mirrored His kindness and wisdom. One of those people was my spiritual director—someone who turned out to be God's voice when I needed it most. Through our conversations, I began to see little glimmers of hope. He gently reminded me of all the prayers that had been answered, urging me to remember the times when I could feel God's grace wrapping around me. Each little blessing painted a picture of God's love and faithfulness that I had momentarily forgotten.

There were indeed times when my prayers seemed to vanish into silence, and I couldn't help questioning if I was worthy of His attention. Finding my way back to faith wasn't straightforward; I had to confront my doubts and fears head-on. My spiritual director encouraged me to be patient and to ease back into my relationship with God. He spoke about timing—how God's schedule often doesn't align with mine but is always perfect in its own way. He reminded me that not every prayer gets a "yes," and sometimes the silence is an answer, too.

As I reflected on his insights, something started stirring in my heart—a desire to reconnect with God. I found myself praying not only for the things I wanted but also for the strength to trust His plan. I won't lie; there were times my faith faltered, and I worried I was losing my grip on what gives my life meaning. In those uncertain moments, I prayed earnestly for God to draw me closer. I needed His grace to learn patience, to accept His timing, and to trust that His ways are often beyond my understanding.

Slowly but surely, I began to see how all my experiences, both good and bad, were woven into a tapestry of growth. I realized that even during my moments of doubt, God was crafting something beautiful within me. It was comforting to know that when I reached out to Him, He did respond, even if His answers sometimes came in unexpected ways. Coming to the realization that I was never abandoned was a profound moment. It reminded me that I'm not alone in my struggles—that He is right beside me, guiding me on this faith journey.

Now, as I continue down this path, I'm much more aware of the blessings surrounding me and the grace shared not just with me but with my loved ones, too. My heart swells with gratitude for every answered prayer, big and small, and I find myself humbled for the times I've questioned His plans. I want to cultivate a deeper trust—a quiet confidence that, even when I don't understand, I am always cared for.

I hope to always remember to call on Him, to seek His presence in every moment, and to remain open to the incredible and unsearchable things He wants to share with me. With each prayer, I embrace the hope of feeling His embrace a little tighter, knowing He's always there, ready to guide and support me.

Dear God,

As I sit in quiet reflection, I want to first take a moment to express my deep gratitude for all that You have provided me. Thank You for the gift of life, for the love of my family and friends, and for the simple joys that fill my days. I recognize that each blessing comes from You, and I am so incredibly grateful.

Lord, I come to You with a heart that's sometimes heavy. There are moments when I feel overwhelmed by the challenges I face—whether it's in my personal life, my work, or my relationships. Please help me to navigate these difficulties with grace and strength. Remind me that I am never alone and that Your presence is always with me, guiding me through the storms.

In times of uncertainty, grant me clarity and focus. Help me to resist the urge to rush ahead and instead to pause and seek Your guidance. Teach me patience as I wait for Your answers and give me the faith to trust in Your timing.

I also ask for Your healing touch, Lord. If there are wounds within me—past hurts or current struggles—I lay them before You. Please help me to let go of bitterness and resentment and to embrace forgiveness, both for myself and for others. I long for a lighter heart and a spirit that radiates Your peace.

Lord, I want to be a beacon of Your love in this world. Help me to see those around me who may be hurting or in need. Open my eyes to opportunities to serve others, whether through kind words, acts of compassion, or simply being present. May my actions reflect Your light and inspire others to seek You as well.

Thank You for Your unwavering love and for the hope that fills my heart. I am grateful for the moments when I feel Your presence most strongly, and I pray for more of those experiences so that I can grow closer to You. Please continue to mold me into the person You want me to be, guiding my steps along the path of righteousness.

In all that I do, may I honor You and bring glory to Your name. Thank You for always being there for me, even when I stray. I trust in Your forgiveness and promise to keep striving to walk in Your light.

Amen.

Burdens to Blessings

"Come to me, all you who are weary and burdened, and I will give you rest. Take my yoke upon you and learn from me, for I am gentle and humble in heart, and you will find rest for your souls. For my yoke is easy and my burden is light."

(Matthew 11:28-30)

Balancing the roles of being a mom, a working woman, and a wife often feels like an enormous challenge that can become overwhelming. There are days when the responsibilities weigh heavily on my shoulders, pressing down on my spirit. In those moments, I find solace in the words that resonate within me: "Come to me, all you who are weary and burdened, and I will give you rest." This promise is my anchor, a reminder of the divine support that surrounds me amidst the chaos of daily life.

My typical day is a whirlwind of activity. Mornings start with the rush of getting my daughter ready for school while trying to find a moment for myself, often just enough time for a quick cup of coffee. The chores never seem to end—laundry piles up, cleaning the house, and schedules must be coordinated. Each task feels like a duty but managing them all can feel like a delicate balancing act. Add in the demands of my job and the need to nurture my relationship with my spouse, and it can sometimes feel like I'm spinning in circles.

In those chaotic times, I've learned the importance of sharing my burdens with God. It's a liberating realization that I don't have to carry everything alone; it's okay to seek support and share my struggles. Spending time in prayer has become my sanctuary, a sacred space to release my feelings and reflect on the often unrealistic expectations I set for myself and those around me. I'm learning that it's okay to be imperfect and that asking for help doesn't indicate weakness.

One of the most important lessons I've embraced is prioritizing self-care without guilt. My physical and spiritual rest has become essential for my overall well-being. Those quiet moments after my daughter falls asleep are precious, allowing me to savor stillness and recharge my spirit. Nature walks provide a sense of peace as I breathe in the fresh air, reminding me of life's simple joys. Prayer becomes a quiet conversation where I lay down my burdens and reconnect with the divine.

Practicing gentleness and humility has transformed my interactions with my family. I strive to approach them with compassion and patience. It's often challenging but reminding myself that I can lean on the support of friends and fellow believers lifts the weight off my heart. Jesus' words, "My yoke is easy, and my burden is light," serve as a mantra, reframing my roles as rewarding challenges that foster growth.

By intentionally carving out time for self-care and spiritual nourishment, I find myself creating beautiful, joyful moments with my family. Life will continue to present burdens but finding rest and embracing support build resilience. My faith has become my strength, empowering me to face challenges. I hold onto the knowledge that I'm part of a larger story intertwined with God's grace and love.

As I live each day, I strive to cultivate a fulfilling life. I want to transform my burdens into lessons, each teaching me more about who I am as a mother, a professional, and a partner—rooted deeply in Christ's love and guidance. This perspective enhances my well-being and shapes my identity, reflecting not only the struggles I face but also the grace accompanying me on this journey.

Dear God,

In the chaos of being a working mom and a wife, I often feel overwhelmed and weary. Yet I hold onto Your promise: "Come to me, all you who are weary and burdened, and I will give you rest." This reminder helps me find strength in my daily struggles. Lord, with the demands of family and work weighing on me, I recognize that I sometimes set unrealistic expectations. Help me embrace my imperfections, ask for help, and prioritize self-care without guilt. Teach me to find moments of rest in my routine, whether through quiet reflection or time in nature so that I can reconnect with my true self. As I navigate my roles, let me approach my family with gentleness and humility. May I lean into patience and remember that I'm not alone; I have a loving community to support me. Help me shift my perspective, seeing motherhood and work as rewarding challenges that foster growth. I seek to carve out time for prayer and spiritual nourishment, cherishing moments of laughter and meaningful connection with my loved ones. While life may never be free of burdens, I trust that by leaning on my faith and embracing Your guidance, I can find resilience and fulfillment.

Amen.

DETAILS MATTER

"If you believe, you will receive whatever you ask for in prayer."

(Matthew 21:22)

Days before my MRI-guided biopsy, I found myself reaching out to a dear friend who is also a doctor. I didn't share details; just simply asked him to pray for me on a specific day. His response was immediate and heartfelt: "What's happening that day?"

With a heavy heart, I finally opened up about the biopsy and the flood of fear that washed over me, particularly the thought of what it could mean for my little girl. The idea of her losing her mother was almost too much to bear.

When I sent him the findings from my previous MRI, I felt a wave of relief knowing that he understood what I was going through. As he reviewed the report, his words became a soothing balm to my anxious soul. "It looks like nothing serious," he reassured me. "They just want to confirm whether it's benign or malignant." He promised to keep me in his prayers, and I knew he meant it sincerely. Had I not been specific with my prayer request and shared the details of my situation, I might have continued to be consumed by worry until the day of the biopsy. That kind of anxiety can eat away at you, bit by bit, if you let it.

At that moment, I felt peace replacing my anxiety. His sincerity and care were a reminder that I wasn't alone in this. It struck me then how vital it is to be specific in our prayers. God knows our hearts, but He invites us to lay our fears and hopes before Him. There's no need for pretense; we can come to Him and say exactly what we're feeling— "Lord, I am scared," or "Lord, help me."

This experience nudged me to reflect on how often I've held back in prayer, thinking I needed the right words or that my concerns were too trivial. But God is involved in every facet of our lives, large or small. He asks us to come with a childlike faith, believing that He is listening and walking alongside us in every trial.

As I waited for the biopsy results, I continued to pray, pouring out my deepest fears and aspirations into the silence. I took comfort in knowing my loved ones, especially my husband, daughter, brothers, mom, best friend, and in-laws, were all praying for me too. Their love became a tangible expression of God's presence in my life.

When the results finally came back benign, I was overwhelmed with relief and gratitude. That moment strengthened my faith and deepened my understanding of how important it is to be transparent in prayer and share our burdens with one another.

I learned that every detail truly matters. Whether you're grappling with a health scare or navigating a difficult decision, remember that God is listening and cares for you deeply. By being honest in our prayers, we allow His grace to unfold in our lives in ways we might not expect. It's a beautiful reminder that we are never truly alone and can always turn to Him, regardless of what we're facing.

Dear God,

I come to you with a heart full of gratitude and humility. In the shadows of fear and uncertainty, You are my refuge and strength. Thank You for the incredible gift of prayer and the privilege of sharing with You the hopes and burdens of my heart.

You understand the worries that can overwhelm us. When doubt creeps in, I'm reminded of Your unwavering love and care. I feel so grateful for the people You have placed in my life who comfort and uplift me, reminding me that I'm surrounded by love and support. Their prayers and encouragement are tangible signs of Your presence in my life.

Lord, I appreciate the lesson You've taught me about the power of being specific in my prayers. You know each detail of my life, yet You desire my honesty and openness. Help me to approach You with a sincere heart and the willingness to be vulnerable, trusting that You hear me and care deeply about every part of my journey.

I confess my fears and anxieties, laying them at Your feet. Thank You for Your forgiveness, mercy, and grace. I love You, and I trust in Your perfect plan for my life. Help me to continue expressing my feelings openly, knowing that You are with me always.

In moments of waiting and uncertainty, I have solace in the knowledge that I'm not alone. The prayers of my loved ones are lifted up alongside mine. Their support reminds me of Your faithfulness and love.

Thank You for Your healing touch and for the peace that surpasses understanding. I'm grateful for the relief and joy that come from trusting in You. Through this journey, my faith has only been strengthened, teaching me the value of being open and honest with You in my prayers.

I pray for anyone who is walking through similar fears and uncertainties. May they find strength and comfort in Your presence. Remind us all that we are never alone and can freely share our burdens with You. Help us to trust in Your goodness and the wonderful plan You have for each of our lives.

Amen.

DIVINE PROVIDENCE

"And we know that in all things God works for the good of those who love him, who have been called according to his purpose."

(Romans 8:28)

Reflecting on my younger years in the convent, I am often filled with gratitude for the invaluable lessons our formators instilled in us. They emphasized the importance of trusting in God's love and providence, urging us not to worry about life's uncertainties. These teachings became a cornerstone for me, shaping my worldview and faith in profound ways.

I vividly remember the day I accepted my first job in the United States—a milestone that felt both exhilarating and daunting. I joined an organization dedicated to saving babies' lives and offering young mothers the shelter and support they desperately needed. The role was more than just providing services; it was about nurturing souls, empowering young people to make positive choices, and inviting them to experience God's love.

During my interview, I learned that the organization relied heavily on God's providence, sustained by private donations and the goodwill of generous supporters. This reliance on divine support resonated deeply with me. I felt a mix of apprehension and excitement, not fully aware of what lay ahead but deeply assured that God would be with me in this new chapter of my life. Reflecting on that moment, I remember how my heart swelled with hope and determination. I took a leap of faith, believing that as I dedicated myself to His work, I would never be alone.

This journey has repeatedly reminded me of my time in the convent. The challenges I faced only solidified my trust in God's love and providence. Each step of this journey has been a testament to the beautiful ways God provides, often through the kindness and generosity of others. Even in moments of doubt and uncertainty, I've learned to cling tightly to His promises. It's comforting to know that God never abandons me; instead, He continues to guide and support me through every trial.

I recall the early days of my job, feeling overwhelmed by the enormity of the mission ahead. Yet, in those moments of doubt, I was reminded of the teachings from the convent. Trusting in God's love and providence became my anchor. I witnessed firsthand how God's provision manifested through the generosity of benefactors and the collective effort of the community. Each donation and each act of kindness reinforced my belief that God's hand was at work, guiding and supporting us.

One particular memory stands out—my first major fundraising event with the organization. The preparations were intense, and I felt the weight of responsibility on my shoulders. But as the day unfolded, I witnessed an outpouring of generosity and support from the community. It was a humbling experience seeing how people came together for a cause rooted in God's love. The event was a success, not just in terms of funds raised but in the sense of unity and shared purpose it fostered.

As I navigate through life, whether in the familiar halls of the convent or here in the vibrant landscape of the United States, I feel God's unwavering presence. This trust has become the cornerstone of my faith, reminding me that as long as I rely on Him, I am walking in the right direction. My journey is not just about fulfilling a mission; it's about deepening my relationship with God and experiencing the remarkable ways He shows up in my life. Each challenge is a reminder of His love and a chance for me to witness His providence in action.

In my quieter moments, I often reflect on these experiences, drawing strength and inspiration from them. I've learned that trusting in God doesn't mean life will be free of challenges, but it means knowing that I am never alone in facing them. This journey has taught me the value of faith, the power of community, and the beauty of God's providence. It's a journey I am grateful for, one that continues to shape me and deepen my faith every day.

Dear God,

In the quiet moments of my heart, I come before You, reflecting on the journey You've guided me through. I think back to my time in the convent, where I truly learned the importance of trusting in Your love and providence. Those lessons have become a part of who I am, and I hold them close to my heart.

As I navigate my path forward, I ask for Your help in clinging to those teachings, especially when the way ahead feels uncertain or intimidating. Life can throw challenges my way that seem tough to overcome, and during those times, I really need Your guidance. Remind me that I'm never alone in anything I take on; Your presence is the light that guides me, even when things feel dark.

Please fill me with courage when fear starts to take over my thoughts and help me see beyond the obstacles I face. I need Your strength to keep pushing forward, especially when I feel like giving up. Let me remember that any setbacks I encounter can serve as a chance for growth instead of despair.

Lord, help me be a vessel of Your love. I want to bring everyone I meet closer to You. Let my actions be a reflection of Your kindness so that others may feel Your love through me. I hope I can find ways to lift those around me, offering support in their times of need, just as You've supported me. May Your providence flow through me, making a positive impact in the lives I touch.

I want to trust in Your plan, even when I can't see where it's leading me. Give me the strength to embrace the purpose You've laid out for me. I know that my understanding is limited, but I aim to remain patient and faithful. Help me to let go of my worries and to place my trust in You, believing that You have a greater vision for my life.

Thank You for being a constant source of comfort and strength. I'm grateful for the many blessings You've given me and the love that surrounds me. I surrender my fears and anxieties into Your hands, resting in the assurance of Your everlasting love.

As I take each step forward, I want my heart to be open, my spirit resilient, and my mind receptive to the guidance of Your Holy Spirit Help me embrace every moment with gratitude and purpose, recognizing the sacredness of each day. Thank You for hearing my prayer. I trust that You'll lead me in ways beyond my understanding.

Amen.

Embracing the Gift of Love: Reflections on the Birth of Jesus

"⁷and she gave birth to her firstborn, a son. She wrapped him in cloths and placed him in a manger because there was no guest room available for them.

⁸And there were shepherds living out in the fields nearby, keeping watch over their flocks at night. ⁹An angel of the Lord appeared to them, and the glory of the Lord shone around them, and they were terrified.¹⁰But the angel said to them, "Do not be afraid. I bring you good news that will cause great joy for all the people.¹¹Today in the town of David a Savior has been born to you; he is the Messiah, the Lord.¹²This will be a sign to you: You will find a baby wrapped in cloths and lying in a manger."

¹³Suddenly, a great company of the heavenly host appeared with the angel, praising God and saying,¹⁴"Glory to God in the highest heaven, and on earth peace to those on whom his favor rests."

(Luke 2:7-14)

Reflecting on the birth of Jesus always brings me a deep sense of peace and hope that I truly cherish. However, one particular Christmas season stands out in my memory as a pivotal moment that transformed my understanding of the nativity story and how I approach my own life.

That year, life felt like a whirlwind. Work pressures were mounting, and I was facing personal struggles that left me feeling overwhelmed. I remember rushing through the holiday season, checking off boxes on my to-do list, but all the while, I felt a void—something essential was missing amidst the chaos. Desperate for some quiet, I decided to attend a Christmas Eve service at a local church. I hoped that within those walls, I might find a refuge from the hustle and bustle.

Walking into the softly lit sanctuary, I was instantly enveloped by the warm glow of candlelight and the soothing sounds of familiar carols. It felt like stepping into another world. At that moment, my heart began to calm, and I could feel a weight lifting off my shoulders. As the nativity story was read aloud, I found myself transported to that humble stable in Bethlehem. I could almost see the stars shining brightly above, and I was reminded that extraordinary events often unfold in the most ordinary of places.

What resonated with me profoundly was the realization that true greatness is found in love, humility, and the simple act of serving others—qualities that seem to be overshadowed by our pursuit of wealth and status. I became acutely aware of how busy I had allowed my life to become, and it struck me how vital it was to slow down and appreciate the relationships that truly matter. I thought about the shepherds—those unassuming men who were the first to hear the good news of Jesus' birth. They were out in the fields, tending to their flocks, just like I often found myself caught up in the daily grind. This reflection stirred a sense of gratitude in me for the everyday blessings that I often took for granted.

As I listened, I found comfort in knowing that God's love is unconditional and reaches each and every one of us, regardless of where we are in life. It encouraged me to open my heart to others, to be more compassionate, and to recognize that everyone is on their own journey, often facing struggles I may not see. The journey of the wise men also captured my thoughts. Their quest for wisdom and the gifts they brought felt like a gentle nudge for me to give my very best to the world. It inspired me to pursue a deeper understanding and to serve others with a heart full of compassion rather than obligation.

Leaving the church that night, I felt a lightness in my spirit that I hadn't felt in a long time. The experience rekindled a realization within me: the essence of Christmas lies not in material things or frantic preparations but in those quiet moments of reflection and the love we share with one another. The birth of Jesus symbolizes hope and new beginnings, a reminder to carry that spirit in my actions and interactions throughout the year.

This profound experience stays with me, inspiring me to embody compassion and love in my daily life. I strive, especially during the Christmas season, to reconnect with that message and let it guide my decisions. Even as life throws challenges my way, I hold onto that light and hope, grateful for its guidance and the strength it gives me to navigate through tough times. Each Christmas, I find myself reflecting on that sacred night, using it as a compass to steer me back to what truly matters—love, kindness, and the simple yet profound joy of being present for others.

Dear God,

As I take a moment to think about the miraculous birth of Jesus, my heart fills with gratitude and reverence. This sacred season reminds me of the incredible gift of hope that His arrival brought to the world. Thank You for sending Your Son to light up our lives, teaching us what love, humility, and kindness really mean.

In a world that often feels chaotic and overwhelming, I realize that true greatness isn't about status or material possessions but about the compassion we show each other. In the busyness of life, with all its responsibilities and distractions, I ask for Your guidance to help me slow down.

Teach me to appreciate the blessings that surround me every day—the warmth of family, the laughter of friends, and the beauty of nature.

Help me find joy in the little things, just like the shepherds and wise men found wonder in the humble birth of the Savior. Their journey to pay homage wasn't about their status but their willingness to seek and recognize the light in unexpected places.

Lord, please guide me to embody the compassion You showed through Jesus. In my interactions with loved ones, colleagues, and even strangers help me reflect the love and faith demonstrated by those who first witnessed Christ's birth. May I approach every encounter with an open heart, ready to listen, understand, and serve. Give me the wisdom to lift those who are struggling and to offer comfort and support to those in need.

When I feel overwhelmed by stress and chaos, I pray for the stillness that allows me to reconnect with the true essence of Christmas. In moments of silence, remind me that it's through reflection and gratitude that I find true joy. Help me make time in my busy schedule for contemplation and prayer so I can grow in my relationship with You and others.

As I carry the spirit of Christmas into each day, help me be a beacon of Your love and light. Let my actions and words reflect Your grace and kindness. Inspire me to reach out to those who may feel lost, isolated, or forgotten so I can share the hope that entered the world through Jesus. Remind me that every small act of kindness counts and can make a big difference in someone's life.

Thank You, Lord, for Your unconditional love that surrounds and sustains us all. May I always be aware of Your blessings and strive to share them with others so that together, we can light up the world with the glow of Your love. As we celebrate this holy season, may my heart stay open to the lessons of humility, grace, and love that Christmas embodies.

Amen.

FAITH SHADED WITH UNCERTAINTY

"Why, my soul, are you downcast? Why so disturbed within me? Put your hope in God, for I will yet praise him, my Savior and my God."

(Psalm 42:11)

When my dad died of cardiac arrest, my heart shattered. It's hard to admit, but in moments of deep pain, my faith often feels shaken. I can still remember the moments right after his passing—the shock, the grief, the overwhelming sense of loss. It was as if part of me was taken away. I found myself questioning God more than ever in those dark hours: "Lord, I don't understand. Why did You allow the death of someone who meant so much to me? Why did You take away my dad?" The questions just kept coming. "Have You turned Your back on me? Do You care about my pain?" Those doubts felt like heavy weights on my soul, leaving me feeling abandoned. I know I shouldn't question His ways, especially during trials, but it's really tough when the pain feels unbearable. Still, deep down, I know God has been good to me in many ways, even in my doubt. I remember times when He provided comfort and strength. Those memories give me hope. While God's Word might not erase my sadness, I find comfort in knowing He is wise, good, and Almighty. He sees my pain, even when I can't grasp His plan. As I navigate through my grief, I remind myself that He is with me, guiding me. I hold onto the truth that He is my Savior and God and that I can still offer Him praise even in my doubt. I understand that this journey of faith mixed with doubt is part of my growth. Each day, I look for moments of peace and trust in God's greater plan, even when it's hard to see. I'm grateful for how He has shaped my life and for the strength He offers, even in the darkest times.

Dear God,

As I come before You today, my heart feels heavy with all the emotions I've been carrying. It's not easy to face the pain of loss and the questions that swirl in my mind. I want to take a moment to express my gratitude for Your presence in my life, especially during these challenging times. You are always with me, even when the road feels dark and uncertain.

Lord, I'm reaching out for Your comfort. I'm struggling to make sense of my grief, and sometimes it feels overwhelming. I miss my dad so much; the ache in my heart is constant. Please wrap Your arms around me and soothe my sorrow. Help me to remember the beautiful moments we shared and the love that still connects us, even though he is no longer here. Let me find peace in those memories and know he is safe in Your embrace.

I often wonder why things happen the way they do. I find myself questioning, "Why did You allow this?" I know I shouldn't question Your ways, but it's hard not to be in my moments of weakness. I ask that You give me the strength to face these doubts and understand that You have a purpose, even when I can't see it. Please help me to lean on my faith, even when it feels shaken. Please remind me of the countless ways You have shown Your goodness in my life. Thinking back to the times You provided for me, supported me, and lifted me up from my lowest points brings me hope.

I know that I can find comfort in Your Word, and I ask that You help me to seek it more earnestly. Let the truths in Scripture be a refuge for my weary soul, guiding me through the darkness and filling my heart with peace. I also pray for those who are grieving and struggling alongside me. May they find comfort in Your presence, and may we support one another on this journey. Help us share our burdens and hold onto the hope of knowing

You. Give us the strength to be there for each other, providing love and encouragement in this difficult time.

As I navigate this path of grief, please help me to recognize the moments of beauty and grace that still exist around me. Teach me to find joy in the small things and to celebrate the life and love that continues to surround me. I want to cultivate a spirit of gratitude even amid the pain. Let my heart be open to Your healing and guide me towards the light You provide.

Above all, Lord, I trust in Your plan. I trust that you are working on all things for good, even when I can't understand how. Help me to place my hope in You daily, guiding my steps and holding me close as I walk this road. Thank You for being my Savior, my refuge, and my comforter. In Jesus name, I pray.

Amen.

Finding Value Beyond Recognition

²⁸*"The older brother became angry and refused to go in. So his father went out and pleaded with him.²⁹But he answered his father, 'Look! All these years, I've been slaving for you and never disobeyed your orders. Yet you never gave me even a young goat so I could celebrate with my friends.³⁰But when this son of yours who has squandered your property with prostitutes comes home, you kill the fattened calf for him!'*

³¹*"'My son,' the father said, 'you are always with me, and everything I have is yours.³²But we had to celebrate and be glad because this brother of yours was dead and is alive again; he was lost and is found.'"*

(Luke 15:28-32)

Reflecting on the older son in the Parable of the Prodigal Son, I can't help but see my own journey in his story. I've often found myself in the role of the dependable one—always in the background, committed to fulfilling my responsibilities while watching those around me take bold steps into the world. I'm the one quietly supporting, always doing what's expected, and never voicing a complaint. Yet, as I carry out my duties, I can't shake the feeling of being overlooked.

This role can be a heavy burden. While others venture out, embrace freedom, and learn through their mistakes, I remain firmly anchored in my responsibilities, often feeling as if my sacrifices go unnoticed. When the younger brother returns home, rejoicing and basking in the warmth of a celebration, it strikes me deeply. It's hard to swallow when all the hard work and dedication I've shown feel eclipsed by his return. Woven into my resentment is a profound sense of invisibility—like every ounce of effort I've poured in has vanished into thin air.

I remember a specific time when one of my colleagues was experiencing life's highs—promotion and pay raise—while I was busy managing day-to-day responsibilities, often sacrificing my own desires and ambitions. Seeing that person celebrated, I felt the sting of belittlement; the contrast between their joyous exploration and my seemingly stagnant path was hard to bear. It wasn't just about jealousy—it was a deeper ache of feeling underappreciated for my reliability and loyalty.

Then, there's the moment in the parable when the father turns to the older son and speaks words of love and affirmation: "Everything I have is yours." It hit me square in the heart. I began to recognize that my quiet contributions, my willingness to hold steady, and my dedication have their own kind of value. The father's gentle reminder that his love for the older son is unwavering, regardless of the younger brother's return, resonates with me deeply. It's a poignant nudge that my worth doesn't hinge on loud celebrations or flashy achievements; love is not a scarce resource that diminishes when shared with others.

In that moment, I confronted the bitterness I'd been harboring—not just towards others who seem to glide through life but also towards myself for feeling trapped in jealousy and self-righteousness. It challenges me to consider embracing forgiveness. Love isn't a competition. The joy of others doesn't negate the love I receive. Instead, it can inspire a communal sense of joy where everyone's journey is valued.

As I reflect on this parable, I see how much it mirrors my life. It's helped me recognize that I need to find joy in my own path, embracing my consistent support and love, even if they don't always get the spotlight. I realize now that I carry the potential to celebrate others' successes without it feeling like a loss for me. Just as I'd hope for a warm welcome if I ever lost my way, I can extend that same grace and joy to others.

This reflection serves as a powerful call to broaden my perspective. Love and grace are abundant; they're not meant to be held tightly or kept in check. I'm inspired to let go of grudges, celebrate the journeys of those who've strayed, and share in this wealth of love generously. Stepping outside of my own narrative, I can embrace the idea that there is room for everyone to thrive, all while learning to appreciate my unique contributions along the way.

Dear God,

As I reflect on the story of the older son in the Parable of the Prodigal Son, I come before You with a heart open to understanding my own journey. I see pieces of myself in this son—always dependable, always present, pouring my efforts into my responsibilities while watching others take risks and stray. Lord, it can be challenging to bear witness to celebrations of those who wander when I feel unseen and unappreciated in my steadfastness. Help me to recognize the moments of resentment that arise in my heart. I ask for Your grace to soften those feelings, to transform my bitterness into compassion. Remind me that every act of loyalty and hard work is not in vain, for You value each of us uniquely. May I find solace in Your reassuring words, knowing that I am loved and that my contributions matter to You. Teach me to embrace forgiveness—not just for the mistakes of others, but for my own feelings of inadequacy and self-righteousness. Help me to see that love is not a finite resource; there is enough to go around. Let me rejoice in the redemption of others, understanding that it does not diminish my own worth in Your eyes. Lord, guide me as I seek to find joy in my own path. May I always recognize Your unwavering love and faithfulness in my life, even when it feels overshadowed. Help me to release any grudges that weigh heavy on my heart and to genuinely celebrate the return of those who have lost their way, just as I would hope for my own welcome. Open my heart to Your abundant love and grace, Lord. Teach me to share it freely, knowing that Your love multiplies as it spreads. I thank You for Your constant presence and for reminding me of the beauty found in both the steady and the wayward journeys.

Amen.

Following the Crucified: A Vocation Story

"For whoever wants to save their life will lose it, but whoever loses their life for me and for the gospel will save it."

(Mark 8:35)

During Jesus' lifetime, He had many followers as long as He was healing their diseases, feeding them, and comforting them. However, when He spoke of deeper spiritual truths, like taking up their cross daily, many turned away. In this Gospel, Jesus presents the requirements for following Him: dedication at any cost, detachment, and prompt renunciation. This resonates deeply with my own vocation story.

All my life, I wanted to follow Jesus and serve Him, though it has been a struggle. I recall the many times I delayed answering His call. The first time was during my senior year of high school when I said, "Yes, Lord, but let me finish college first." The second time, after college, I said, "Yes, Lord, but let me experience a career first." I found a job in Cebu, Philippines, and attended a Vocation Formation Encounter, thinking, "Lord, aren't You tired of calling me?" I participated in the encounter but didn't accept His invitation to follow Him. I tried to convince myself that I didn't have a vocation for religious life. I believed I could still serve Him without becoming a religious. I loved my comforts and had many dreams for myself and my family. How could I have all these if I entered religious life? I bargained with God, offering to serve Him as a layperson. But He never stopped calling me until I finally surrendered, saying, "Yes, Lord, no buts, no ifs."

I remember vividly the moment I realized I could no longer run from His call. I was sitting alone in my room, feeling the weight of my decisions and the emptiness that came from resisting what I knew deep down was my true path. The stillness of that night was broken by a profound sense of peace that washed over me. I knew then that following Jesus meant more than just attending church on Sundays or living a good life; it meant dedicating myself entirely to His service, no matter the cost.

I know that following Him is not easy. It involves following a crucified Christ. It requires detachment and total surrender, and it means being ready to be misunderstood and scorned. Yet, because of my deep love for the Lord, I found the strength to follow Him. I had to be ready to lose face and to give up the easy, socially acceptable way of being a Christian. If young people had known the demands of true discipleship in Jesus, many would have gladly chosen Christ, embracing His Gospel message and modeling their lives after Him.

The youth today seek real challenges. That is why so many of them are leaving their comfortable lives at home and joining others who live demanding lives of renunciation. Discipleship is for all Christians, not just those with special vocations. It's a demanding path, but with Christ as our faithful companion, we can be assured of His constant presence.

Let us entrust our lives to Him with total confidence, knowing He is always with us on our journey of faith.

Dear God,

As I sit here in quiet reflection, I want to take a moment to say thank you for Your unwavering love and for calling me to follow You. Your presence in my life has been a guiding light, helping me navigate the paths I sometimes find difficult. I'm grateful for Your patience throughout my journey, especially when I hesitated or tried to turn away from the understanding and commitment You invite me to. I recognize that fear and uncertainty have sometimes clouded my judgment, leading me astray. Yet, your grace has always brought me back, gently reminding me of Your consistent love.

As I move forward, I ask for the courage to embrace the challenges that come with being a true disciple. Help me to take up my cross daily and to let go of the comforts and distractions that keep me from living a life devoted to You. I don't want to be caught up in the fleeting desires of this world. Instead, please instill in me a spirit of perseverance and faithfulness so that I can truly focus on being wholly Yours. Teach me to say "Yes" without conditions, to trust in the plans You've laid out for me, knowing they are far better than anything I could come up with.

As I tread my path in this uncertain world, remind me that I am not alone in this journey. Surround me with Your love and guidance and help me stay strong in responding to Your call with an open heart. Grant me the courage to stand firm in my faith, even when it means losing face in the eyes of others. I want to be a light to those around me—especially those searching for authenticity and purpose in all the confusion.

Help me reflect on Your teachings in my actions so my life can be a testament to Your transformative power. Guide me daily as I strive to embody compassion, humility, and kindness. When I encounter those who are lost or struggling, give me the right words, gestures, and understanding. Help me meet their needs in small ways so that they can catch a glimpse of Your unconditional love through me.

As I submit my plans and hopes to You, keep my heart focused on You. I trust You with my life, knowing You will be with me in every moment—whether in joy or sorrow, triumph or struggle. Let Your presence be my peace and strength, guiding me through every challenge. With You by my side, I'm confident I can overcome anything, and I look forward to seeing how You work in my life and through me for the sake of others. Thank You for the sacred journey we share. May I grow closer to You each day, learning to love and serve as You do.

Amen.

FOR THIS CHILD, I PRAYED

"²⁷I prayed for this child, and the Lord has granted me what I asked of him.²⁸So now I give him to the Lord. For his whole life, he will be given over to the Lord." And he worshiped the Lord there."

(1 Samuel 1:27-28)

From the very beginning, my heart was set on having a family. Growing up, I always envisioned myself surrounded by children, creating a loving and nurturing home filled with laughter and joy. When I got married, this dream became even more vivid and real. I was excited to start this new chapter of life with my husband, and we both shared the desire to have a child. However, as I entered my 40s, I knew that having a child might be more challenging, but my faith remained strong. I believed that God had a plan for us and that His timing was perfect.

When we found out that we were pregnant, I was ecstatic. I couldn't contain my excitement and immediately set up an appointment to see an OB-GYN. However, my joy quickly turned to heartbreak during our first appointment. The doctor told us that there was no baby showing in the ultrasound, only a sac. She said we needed to arrange a D&C to remove the tissue from my uterus. I was in shock. My husband and I sat in the parking lot for a while, trying to process the news. We searched the internet for possible reasons why the ultrasound result was like that and read reviews about the OB-GYN. Many of the reviews were not favorable, which surprisingly gave me hope. I prayed that the doctor had misdiagnosed me.

I questioned God, asking, "Why not give it to me?" I felt ready to be a mother. But I also reminded myself that God's timing is perfect. Everything was hazy, and I couldn't think straight. I kept praying for a child to complete our family. Still, in the parking lot, we searched for another OB-GYN and made an appointment to see her the following week. During that time, I never ceased praying and hoping that the result would be favorable.

When we saw the second OB-GYN, I was filled with anticipation. And yes, I was pregnant with a baby, not just an empty sac. I was pregnant with a baby girl. I couldn't contain my happiness and couldn't stop thanking God for this blessing. Despite the complications and challenges that came with a high-risk pregnancy, I was determined to carry my daughter to term. The due date was moved to an earlier date each time I had my prenatal visits. I had two doctors helping me with my pregnancy to ensure both me and the baby were healthy.

I carried her for 37 weeks, enduring the physical and emotional challenges with unwavering determination. I fought the hardest battles for my child, bore all the pains, and would have given up my life for her. Throughout it all, I prayed for this child, and God heard my prayers.

Raising my daughter has been a rewarding yet challenging journey. Each day, I pray that my husband and I will raise her to be the person God wants her to be. I seek to instill in her the values of faith, love, and service to God. I am reminded of Proverbs 22:6, which says, "Train up a child in the way he should go, and when he is old, he will not depart from it." My faith and commitment to raising her in a godly manner will have a lasting impact on her life, and I trust that she will grow up knowing the love and grace of God.

My story is one of faith, perseverance, and gratitude. It is a testament to the power of prayer and the importance of trusting in God's plan, even when the path seems uncertain.

Dear God,

I come before You with a heart full of gratitude and awe for the miracles You have worked in my life. Lord, You have blessed me with the precious gift of life, and for that, I am eternally grateful. Just as Hannah dedicated Samuel to You, I lift up my child to You now, asking for Your divine guidance and protection over her life.

Father, thank You for the journey that brought her to me, for every moment of uncertainty, and for every prayer answered in Your perfect timing. Your steadfast love and faithfulness have carried me through the trials, and I am humbled by Your mercy and grace.

I pray for my child that she may grow in wisdom and strength, in the knowledge of Your love and truth. May she walk in Your ways, shining as a light in this world and bringing glory to Your name Guide her steps, Lord, and surround her with Your presence. May she find joy and peace in Your arms and seek to serve You with all her heart.

Grant me, as a parent, the wisdom, patience, and love to raise her according to Your will. Help me to be a reflection of Your love and to teach her Your ways. May my home be filled with Your Spirit, a place of faith, hope, and love, where Your name is always honored.

Lord, I surrender my life to You, trusting in Your plan and Your timing. Strengthen my faith so that I may continue to lean on You in every season of life. Thank You for the incredible blessing of my child and Your unending grace.

Amen.

FORGIVE ONE ANOTHER

"Be kind and compassionate to one another, forgiving each other, just as in Christ God forgave you."

(Ephesians 4:32)

Reflecting on my journey, I often find myself grappling with the pain that comes from betrayal. When someone I held dear betrays my trust, it's like a sharp sting that lingers long after the initial hurt. I've had moments when my trust was shattered—it's tough to forgive those who have caused me so much pain. Holding onto grudges felt like a way to protect myself from being hurt again, even though deep down, I knew it wasn't helping me heal. As someone who strives to live according to Christian values, I understand that I'm called to be kind, compassionate, and forgiving. However, aligning my feelings with this calling is a continuous struggle. The disappointment and hurt make it really hard to let go and forgive. In those tough moments, I find some comfort in my faith, reminding myself that God understands my struggles and is walking with me through them. Forgiving is not an easy path, especially when those wounds are still fresh. It takes time to process the hurt and work towards letting go of the resentment that can feel all-consuming. I've learned that it's perfectly okay for me to take my time and acknowledge how difficult it can be to forgive and forget. Forgiveness isn't about excusing what was done to me; it's about freeing myself from the weight of anger and finding my own inner peace. Part of being kind and compassionate includes being gentle with myself. I deserve the time and space to heal. I've come to realize that even small steps, like acknowledging my pain and gradually releasing the anger, can lead to a more profound sense of relief. During these moments of reflection, I lean on my faith and the support from those who truly care about me. Prayer and reading God's word help provide strength and comfort. I trust that God is guiding me through this tough journey, helping me find the courage to forgive. It's a challenging road, but each step I take towards healing is a sign of my resilience and strength. I remind myself to be patient, taking things one day at a time. Ultimately, forgiveness is a gift I'm giving to myself, and I understand that it's a process that requires both time and faith.

Dear God,

I come to You today with a heart that feels heavy and in need of Your compassionate touch. Life can be so challenging, and I often find myself navigating through moments that leave me feeling hurt and betrayed. It's in these moments that I struggle the most. I find myself replaying the pain, allowing it to overshadow the joy and love that I truly desire to feel. Lord, grant me a forgiving and loving heart. Help me to see the good even when others have not treated me kindly. I know that forgiveness is a journey—a path that is sometimes steep and rocky—and yet I want to walk it with You by my side. There are people in my life who have caused me deep pain. Whether it was through betrayal or unkind words, those experiences sit heavily on my heart. It's hard to let go of the ill feelings that arise from these wounds, and I often find myself wrestling with the desire for retribution. I need Your help, God, to release this burden so that I may heal. I know holding onto grudges only robs me of my peace, but letting go feels daunting. Please, God, create in me a heart like Yours—free of hatred and anger. Teach me to acknowledge my feelings without allowing them to dictate my actions. Show me how to express my hurt without bitterness. I'm grateful for the lessons that come with love and trust, even when they're wrapped in hard experiences. Thank You for the joy of loving others and for the pain that teaches me to be wise in my relationships. I long for the strength to forgive those who have hurt me, not because they necessarily deserve it, but because I deserve peace and freedom from the chains of resentment. Each time I find myself stuck in a moment of anger, remind me of the love You extend to me despite all my failures and missteps. Help me understand that just as You forgive me with open arms, I can take steps towards forgiveness with those around me. My compassionate Father, I am profoundly grateful for Your unwavering support and love. You help me see that forgiveness opens the door to healing and allows love to thrive. I often lose sight of the fact that forgiveness isn't just about the other person—it's a precious gift I give to myself. Help me to embrace this truth with an open and willing heart. As I reflect on my relationships, I recognize that there are lessons embedded within the pain. Those who have hurt and betrayed me have also taught me about trust and discernment. I want to become wiser and more cautious about whom I allow into the deeper parts of my heart. Allow these lessons to shape me into someone who loves deeply but also protects their heart wisely. God, I ask for Your healing touch to mend the wounds inside me, to soothe the anger that sometimes bubbles up unexpectedly. Help my heart to expand with compassion, both for others and for myself. Remind me that I, too, am worthy of love and forgiveness despite my own failings. It's in these times of vulnerability that I crave Your presence the most. As I create space for forgiveness in my heart, I humbly ask for the strength to let go. Help me to place my trust in You, knowing that You understand my struggles far more deeply than I express. Each step I take towards forgiveness feels daunting, but with You by my side, I know it is possible. Thank you for listening to my heart and for being my safe sanctuary in times of turmoil. I am learning to let go, one day at a time, finding solace in the love You offer. I pray that with Your guidance, I will step into a future filled with light, love, and genuine relationships. With a heart open to Your transformative love, I offer this prayer.

Amen.

From Isolation to Grace

"7 When a Samaritan woman came to draw water, Jesus said to her, "Will you give me a drink?" 8 (His disciples had gone into the town to buy food.)

9 The Samaritan woman said to him, "You are a Jew and I am a Samaritan woman. How can you ask me for a drink?" (For Jews do not associate with Samaritans.)

10 Jesus answered her, "If you knew the gift of God and who it is that asks you for a drink, you would have asked him, and he would have given you living water."

(John 4:7-10)

Reflecting on the story of the Samaritan Woman at the well, I am reminded of a poignant season in my life that resonates deeply with her journey. There was a time when I felt overwhelmingly disconnected from both myself and those around me—almost as if I were invisible in a crowded room. I found myself wrestling with a decision that burdened my heart, caught in a tempest of emotions that left me feeling isolated. In those moments, I struggled to articulate my pain, and it often felt like no one could truly understand the weight I was carrying.

During that challenging period, a heartfelt conversation with a dear friend became a pivotal moment for me. This friend, embodying the spirit of Christ's love, offered a listening ear without judgment or rushing to provide solutions. In that sacred space, I felt seen and heard in a way I hadn't experienced before—a mirror reflecting back my feelings, validating my struggles. It reminded me so much of the Samaritan Woman's encounter with Jesus, who saw her history and offered her grace. My heart resonated with the refreshing stream of compassion that flowed through our conversation, quenching my thirst for connection and understanding.

At that moment, I recognized the power of compassionate listening as a divine instrument of healing. I was reminded of the scripture that speaks of carrying one another's burdens and fulfilling the law of Christ (Galatians 6:2). I reflected on the truth that everyone carries their own invisible burdens, often hidden beneath the surface. Sometimes, all it takes is for someone to embody Christ's love—to sit quietly with us, listening without judgment—to initiate the healing journey.

Understanding the transformative journey from isolation to belonging has deepened my faith. Just as the Samaritan Woman left her water jar behind to share her story of hope and redemption, I felt compelled to pass on the kindness and understanding that had been shown to me. I wanted to be that safe harbor for someone in need, offering support, love, and empathy, just as Christ offers to us all. This experience opened my eyes to the beautiful call we have as Christians—to reflect God's love in a world that often feels burdened and alone.

Ultimately, it is in these moments of connection—where vulnerability meets understanding—that we truly grasp the essence of community and faith. It is a reminder that, just like the Samaritan Woman, we can encounter Christ in our struggles and emerge empowered to share that love with others, creating a ripple effect of grace and compassion in the lives we touch.

Dear God,

In the quiet moments of my solitude and struggle, I come before You, yearning for solace and strength. Like the Samaritan Woman at the well, I seek Your comforting presence to guide me through the challenges of life. Every drop of uncertainty that weighs upon my heart reminds me of the importance of Your love, which flows infinitely and unconditionally. Grant me the grace to love wholeheartedly, pouring my heart into the relationships that bring me joy and meaning. Help me to embrace not only those who are easy to love but also those who test my patience and understanding.

May I look beyond the surface, recognizing the humanity in everyone I encounter. Teach me, Lord, the art of compassionate listening—an art that requires patience and openness. Allow me to be a source of comfort and a refuge for those who feel burdened and invisible as many wander through life carrying unspeakable worries and pain. Help me create spaces where others can be vulnerable, express their true selves, and find healing in being heard. I pray that my mere presence can bring peace to the troubled and my words can uplift the weary.

In times of difficulty, remind me of the support that surrounds me—friends who listen without judgment and companions who stand beside me, sharing in both my joys and sorrows. May their kindness inspire me to share the gift of understanding and empathy with others, helping to build bridges across divides and bringing warmth to cold interactions. Lord, grant me the courage to reach out to those who may need a gentle nudge of encouragement, filling the gaps with acts of kindness that echo Your love.

Guide me to forgive those who have caused me pain, for I understand that forgiveness is a healing journey, not just for them, but for my own soul. Strengthen my spirit with Your peace and wisdom so that I may navigate life's storms with resilience and grace, finding the silver lining even in the darkest moments. Help me to remember that every challenge is an opportunity for growth and every setback a chance to learn and emerge stronger.

Thank You, Lord, for the moments of connection that illuminate my path. Allow me to cherish the simple joys—a smile shared, a laugh exchanged, and the warmth of a hand held. Help me carry Your light within me, enabling me to share it with others and nurturing a world filled with compassion and love. In this journey of life, may I become an ambassador of Your love, shining brightly in the lives of those around me.

Amen.

GIVE THANKS

"Give thanks in all circumstances, for this is God's will for you in Christ Jesus."

(1 Thessalonians 5:18)

Reflecting on my journey from the Philippines to the United States, I once viewed America as the "land of milk and honey." I thought it was a place full of opportunities where everyone was comfortable and happy. But when I arrived, reality set in. I saw homeless individuals and beggars on the streets, just like in the Philippines. It was a powerful reminder that every country has its struggles and people in need. Witnessing so many people without homes, especially during the harsh winter, I was filled with deep sorrow and empathy. It broke my heart to think about how they managed to survive without shelter to keep them warm. In those moments, I felt a strong connection to their pain, as if God was speaking to me, urging me to recognize the many blessings I have in my life. I realized just how fortunate I am to have a home, a loving family, friends, food to eat, and clothes to wear. These are blessings I often overlook, but seeing others face such hardships opened my eyes to the goodness in my own life. It reminded me to be grateful for what I have and to acknowledge that not everyone is as lucky. This awareness serves as a call to action for me. It pushes me to extend compassion to those less fortunate. Whether it's donating to charity or simply offering a warm meal or a kind word, I believe every small act of kindness can make a difference. It's a way for me to live out my faith and reflect the love and grace I've received. As a Christian, I understand that I'm called to serve others and be a steward of the blessings I've been given. I've learned that every act of service, no matter how small, becomes significant in the eyes of God. By helping those in need, I honor God and fulfill His purpose for my life. Through this experience, I've come to appreciate the importance of gratitude and compassion. It serves as a constant reminder to cherish what I have and to use my blessings to uplift others. I hope to be a beacon of hope and kindness, making a positive impact on the lives of those around me.

Dear God,

Thank you so much for all the countless blessings You have poured into my life. I come before You with a heart full of gratitude, acknowledging the immense love, comfort, and support I have in my family and friends. Help me to never take these gifts for granted and always recognize Your hand in my life.

As I witness the struggles of others, I ask for Your guidance and compassion. Open my eyes and heart to the needs around me. Give me the strength to reach out to those who are less fortunate, to serve them with love and kindness, and to be a source of hope in their lives.

Help me to live out my faith in practical ways, whether through volunteering, sharing my resources, or simply offering a listening ear. Remind me that every small act of service matters and reflects Your love and grace.

Fill me with the courage to act and the wisdom to know how best to help others. May my actions be a testament to Your goodness and a reflection of Your heart.

Thank You for Your endless love and compassion. May I be a vessel of that love to those around me, showing that we are all deserving of kindness and grace.

Amen.

God-Given Talents

"Each of you should use whatever gift you have received to serve others as faithful stewards of God's grace in its various forms."

(1 Peter 4:10)

Looking back on my journey with the Campus Ministry Office at De La Salle University-Dasmariñas, Philippines, I can't help but feel grateful for the incredible impact this community has had on my life. The people I've met and shared experiences with have played a significant role in helping me recognize, accept, and nurture the gifts I believe I've been given. It hasn't always been easy, though; I often struggled with a sense of false humility that made me hesitant to fully embrace those gifts. Being involved in this ministry opened my eyes to the countless blessings I've received from God. For so long, I felt embarrassed to acknowledge my talents and was uncertain about how to put them to good use. However, my Campus Ministry family provided the encouragement and support I needed to cultivate these precious gifts. They helped me see that these talents are not just for my benefit but are meant to serve God's kingdom and those around me. I continue to rely on my faith and the unwavering support of my Campus Ministry family. Their presence reassures me that I'm never alone on this path. Through prayer and turning to God's word, I find the strength and comfort I need. I trust that God is guiding me, helping me to embrace my gifts and use them to serve others. As I forge ahead on this journey, I pray for wisdom, strength, and the grace to serve with an open heart. I've come to understand that no act of service is too small; each one holds significance in the eyes of God. With gratitude and confidence, I aim to create a positive impact in the lives of others by reflecting God's love and grace through everything I do.

Dear God,

I can't help but feel an overwhelming sense of gratitude for the abundant gifts and talents You have bestowed upon me· Each one, unique and precious, has shaped who I am, and for that, I am truly blessed· I often find myself taking these gifts for granted, losing sight of the purpose behind them, and for that, I humbly ask for Your forgiveness· There have been countless moments when I've let my insecurities overshadow the talents You've given me· Times when I hesitated to step forward, to share my skills, or to simply acknowledge their presence in my life· I realize now that in doing so, I not only deny myself but also the joy of sharing Your light with the world around me· I pray that You guide me to harness these gifts not just for my own benefit but as tools to uplift those who cross my path. Let me see each interaction as a chance to reflect Your love, to spread kindness, and to make a difference, no matter how small. I want to cherish the opportunity to impact others positively, reminding myself that my talents are not just for me; they are a shared blessing. Lord, create in me a heart brimming with gratitude. Help me cultivate a spirit eager to serve and willing to step beyond my comfort zone. Let me recognize the true value of these abilities and inspire me to use them wisely, always with love at the forefront of my intentions. I want to embody Your grace and compassion in everything I do, so please strengthen my resolve to be a faithful steward of the gifts You've entrusted to me. Every act of kindness, every moment of service, no matter how seemingly insignificant, is a chance to testify to Your greatness. I pray that through my actions, others may glimpse Your endless love and mercy. Thank You for the beautiful joys and the challenges that come with trusting in You. Each of these moments teaches me more about faith, patience, and love. As I continue on this journey, I will seek to honor You in all that I do. Help me to grow, to learn, and to shine Your light in a world that so desperately needs it.

Amen.

God's Living Witness

"In the same way, let your light shine before others, that they may see your good deeds and glorify your Father in heaven."

(Matthew 5:16)

Aunt Patsy was my husband's aunt, and I had the privilege of knowing her for about five years before she went to be with our Creator. In that short time, she made a profound impact on my life. She was a woman of unwavering principle, prayer, and faith. It's heartbreaking that cancer took her life too soon. I often wish she could have lived longer, continuing to touch lives as she did. She loved my husband as if he were her child, adored my daughter, and welcomed me as a cherished part of their family.

The day of her funeral was bittersweet. Walking into the nearly packed church, I was deeply moved by the sheer number of people who gathered to pay their respects. Aunt Patsy's influence was far-reaching, and it was clear that her love and kindness had touched many hearts. Testimony after testimony painted a picture of a woman wholly devoted to God and serving others.

I learned that Aunt Patsy had a quiet ministry that was powerful in its simplicity. She would leave Bible tracts where people could easily find them—in waiting rooms, restrooms, and even in the tip booklet at restaurants. Her dedication to spreading

God's word was unwavering, and she believed that even the smallest act of sharing faith could make a difference.

One particularly inspiring story shared at her funeral was about how she brought the love and hope of Jesus into the lives of young prisoners. She visited them, shared scriptures, and provided spiritual guidance to those often forgotten by society. Her compassion knew no bounds, and she saw the face of Christ in everyone she encountered.

Aunt Patsy was indeed God's living witness. She lived out His love daily, serving as a beacon of mercy and grace. Her life was a testament to the power of faith, and her legacy continues to inspire those who knew her. She taught me that being a Christian is not just about words but about actions that reflect God's love.

Though Aunt Patsy is no longer with us, her spirit lives on in the countless lives she touched. She was a true instrument of love and mercy, a shining example of how one person can make a remarkable difference in the world. Although she is deeply missed, her memory fills us with hope and a renewed commitment to live out our faith in the same way.

May we all strive to witness God's love as Aunt Patsy did.

Dear God,

I come to You with a humble heart, seeking Your guidance and strength. I want to be a living witness of Your love, grace, and mercy. Help me reflect Your light in everything I do, so others may see Your goodness through my actions and words.

Fill my heart with compassion and kindness, teaching me to love selflessly and serve those in need with a willing spirit. May my life be a testament to Your transformative power and boundless love.

Grant me the courage to share Your word and spread the message of hope and salvation. Give me wisdom to know when to speak and when to listen, guiding others closer to You. Let my actions be a beacon of Your love that draws others into a deeper relationship with You.

Help me to live a life of integrity and faithfulness. Strengthen my faith to stand firm against challenges and trials, trusting in Your perfect plan, knowing You are with me every step of the way.

I ask for Your grace to forgive those who have wronged me and to seek reconciliation where there is division. Let my life reflect Your peace and unity, and may I be an instrument of healing and restoration.

As I go about my daily life, remind me that I am Your ambassador. Help me be mindful of the opportunities You place before me to share Your love and to be a light in the darkness. May my life bring glory to Your name and inspire others to seek You.

Amen.

Holy Love

"Husbands, love your wives, just as Christ loved the church and gave himself up for her."

(Ephesians 5:25)

Growing up with my loving parents, I promised myself that when I got married, I would find a husband like my Papa. From an early age, I witnessed a love story that was both tender and resilient. I watched as my Papa, with unwavering dedication, showered my Mama with love and care. His tireless efforts to provide for our family were not just about meeting our needs but were acts of love that spoke louder than words. My Papa was a devoted husband and a dedicated provider, instilling in us values and principles that have become the bedrock of my life. My Papa was the ideal man, the epitome of what a husband should be, and I knew I wanted a partner who embodied those same qualities.

As I grew older and navigated the tumultuous waters of relationships, I faced several heartbreaks that left me disillusioned and hopeless. Each failed relationship chipped away at my dream of finding my ideal man. Yet, amid the despair, my faith remained steadfast. I never ceased praying to God, asking Him to send me a husband who mirrored the qualities I admired in my Papa—a husband rooted in God's love, just as "Christ loved the church and gave himself up for her." I clung to the belief that God rewards those who wait with faith and patience, and I held onto this hope with all my heart.

Indeed, my faith was not in vain. At the age of 40, a time when many might have given up hope, I met Sean, my husband, who was then my boyfriend. The getting-to-know stage was swift, almost as if our souls recognized each other from the start. I knew he was the one. I had prayed for this man, and when I locked eyes on him, I felt a profound sense of peace and certainty. We got married and were blessed with one child. As our lives intertwined, I saw many of my Papa's qualities in him. My husband is a devoted and loving partner. His good looks and witty personality are just the surface of a deep well of faith and integrity. He is God-fearing and has taken impeccable care of me from the first day of our marriage until now. He provides everything for me and our daughter, embodying the very essence of a sacrificial, Christ-like love.

During my pregnancy, which was fraught with complications, my husband was my rock. He was there for me every step of the way, sharing in my pain and supporting me through every challenge. His unwavering presence and support extended beyond my pregnancy as we faced the numerous aftereffects of my high-risk condition. My husband never left my side. He was my wing when I wanted to give up flying, always there to boost my confidence when I felt drained. If I had to choose another husband, I would choose him again and again, without hesitation.

My husband epitomizes "Christ who loved the Church and gave himself up for her." He has shown me the importance of sacrificial love in our life and relationship. He consistently puts my needs and those of our daughter's before his own, embodying a powerful expression of selflessness and devotion. Just as Christ demonstrated unconditional love and a willingness to prioritize the needs of others, my husband cultivates an atmosphere of mutual care within our marriage. This means being present during challenging times, offering encouragement, and actively listening to my thoughts and feelings.

Moreover, this reflection reminds me that love is not always easy. It requires patience, understanding, and sometimes the courage to set aside personal desires for the relationship's well-being. In doing so, my husband honors me as his wife and strengthens the foundation of our union, fostering a deeper bond that can withstand life's trials.

Ultimately, the love of a husband, modeled after Christ's love, is a source of strength and solace in the journey of marriage. It empowers both partners to grow individually and together, reinforcing the idea that love is a continual choice, a commitment to cherish and uplift one another through all seasons of life.

Dear God,

I come to You with a heart full of gratitude for the incredible gift of marriage and the blessing of having my husband by my side. Thank You for bringing him into my life; he reflects the love and qualities I've admired for as long as I can remember. I'm truly thankful for the way he cares for me, supports me, and loves me unconditionally.

As we continue our journey together, I pray for Your guidance in our marriage. Help us build a relationship that reflects Your love—one that is patient, kind, and selfless. May we always cherish each other and be mindful of each other's needs, placing one another first.

Lord, in the tougher times, I ask for wisdom and understanding. Help us to communicate openly and listen with compassion. When challenges arise, let us find strength in You, allowing Your love to shine through us and reminding us of our commitment to each other.

I also pray for my husband. Please bless him with peace and fill him with strength as he supports our family. Help him see how deeply his love impacts me and our child. May he feel appreciated and loved as we all grow together in faith and unity.

Thank You for the beautiful moments we share and for how our love continues to grow. Remind us every day to choose love, uplift one another, and lean on You as we navigate this journey together. Help us cultivate joy and gratitude in our hearts, celebrating both the big milestones and those small everyday moments that mean so much.

Amen.

LEAD ME LORD

"If any of you lacks wisdom, you should ask God, who gives generously to all without finding fault, and it will be given to you." (James 1:5)

Being a parent is a beautiful journey, but it can also feel a bit daunting. My husband and I knew from the start that we had a significant role in shaping our daughter's life, and honestly, that responsibility can be overwhelming. There are moments when the fear of not being enough creeps in.

Since she was born, my prayers for her have intensified. I often find myself worrying about whether we're doing enough, especially when she doesn't listen or follow our guidance. That fear, particularly regarding her spiritual growth, can be tough. I catch myself thinking, what if she veers away from the truths we're trying to instill in her?

Yet, even amidst those worries, there's a profound comfort in God's promises. It's such a relief to know that if we seek His wisdom, He'll guide us. Proverbs 3:5-6 always brings me back to a calm place: "Trust in the Lord with all your heart and lean not on your own understanding; in all your ways submit to him, and he will make your paths straight." It's reassuring to remember that we're not going through this alone.

For us, the best way to influence her spiritually is by living our faith out loud every day. Actions truly do speak louder than words. Deuteronomy 6:6-7 encourages us to discuss God's commandments at home and during our daily activities, making faith a seamless part of our lives.

Parenting goes beyond just attending to her physical and emotional needs; it's about nurturing her spirit. Whether we are celebrating joyful moments or facing challenges, we strive to show her Christ's love and grace, teaching her to pray and rely on God.

One night, as I watched her peacefully sleep, I felt a rush of love and whispered a heartfelt prayer for her future. I prayed for her to grow into a woman of unwavering faith, inspired by God's wisdom and love. Philippians 4:6-7 reminds us not to be anxious and to present our needs to God, reassuring us that His peace will guard our hearts. That's the peace I want for her.

Through our own doubts and fears, we've come to realize that God's guidance applies to us, too. Each day, we seek His wisdom, which helps strengthen our faith and builds our confidence as parents. We trust that He'll equip us with everything we need to guide our daughter on her spiritual path.

Our deepest hope is that she will come to know the Lord in a personal, meaningful way. We pray that she will cherish the faith we nurture in her and always find strength and comfort in God's presence. Isaiah 41:10 resonates deeply: "Do not be dismayed, for I am your God. I will strengthen you and help you; I will uphold you with my righteous right hand."

Dear God,

Thank You for this incredible gift of parenthood and for trusting us with our daughter's life. This role is both a privilege and a responsibility that we approach with humility and a desire for Your guidance.

We ask for Your wisdom on this journey. Help us lead our daughter with love, patience, and grace. May we be living examples of Your faith in our daily lives, making our home a sanctuary where Your presence is felt, and Your name is honored.

Through times of joy and challenge, guide us in modeling Christ's love, teaching her to pray, and showing her how to lean on Your strength.

In our moments of doubt, we've learned that Your guidance is essential for us as well. Each day we seek You, we feel our faith grow and our confidence as parents strengthen. We trust that You will give us the wisdom and discernment needed to shepherd our daughter on her spiritual journey.

Most importantly, Lord, we hope that our daughter will come to know You deeply and personally. We pray that she will hold onto the faith we nurture within her and find comfort in Your presence throughout her life, feeling Your love guiding her through all of life's ups and downs.

Thank You for hearing our prayers and for being our constant source of strength and wisdom. We place our trust in You and choose to surrender our fears, knowing You are with us every step of the way.

Amen.

LOVE 'TIL IT HURTS...

"Love 'til it hurts" was my battle cry ever since I fell in love with a man I thought was heaven-sent to me. Why do I have to get hurt in loving? What does true love mean?

"⁴ Love is patient, love is kind. It does not envy, it does not boast, it is not proud. ⁵ It does not dishonor others, it is not self-seeking, it is not easily angered, it keeps no record of wrongs. ⁶ Love does not delight in evil but rejoices with the truth. ⁷ It always protects, always trusts, always hopes, always perseveres.⁸ Love never fails. But where there are prophecies, they will cease; where there are tongues, they will be stilled; where there is knowledge, it will pass away."

(1Cor. 13: 4-8)

Seeing the love between elderly couples is incredibly heartwarming. Their relationship isn't perfect, but that's what makes it so beautifully genuine. It's a living example of how love can grow and deepen over time. Watching them support each other, share knowing glances, and enjoy quiet moments together is a touching reminder that true love only strengthens with age. Their love reminds me of God's infinite love and inspires me to strive for a similar deep connection in my own relationships so I will never get tired of loving as I grow in age and wisdom.

My experience of loving "someone" many years ago was not a "fairy tale story" (that we live happily ever after). Having fallen out of love with somebody I loved more than myself was not a decision I regret. I learned much from the experience, though I have to go through a painful process of healing and letting go. Letting go of the person and the relationship was a struggle. In the course of loving, I've been hurt, wounded, and lost. I have loved 'til it hurts! Then, what is love? LOVE IS THE COST OF GIVING! In my own journey of loving, I've learned that real love indeed requires selflessness and a willingness to put someone else's needs above your own. I can give without loving, but I can't truly love without giving. This love asks me to give what I value most: my mind, my soul, my strength, and most especially, my HEART! I thank God for all that has been. After all, it's not my loss. I gained back my old self. It's been quite a while since I was able to gather my shattered pieces. It took me some time to forgive myself for loving more than enough. I thank the person, too, for bringing out the "wounded healer" in me, which, in a sense, is very instrumental in my ministry with the young people who are experiencing what I have experienced. Eventually, I became a stronger person, especially in dealing with matters of the heart. After all, everything passes away; only God's love remains. The pains and the hurts I've gone through have come to an end. Even Jesus experienced pain and hurt in loving. He has loved us more than enough to give His life. He has shown His love through His suffering and death, and since everything passes away, in the end, there is resurrection. Jesus taught me how to love unconditionally without counting the cost through this experience. What consoles me most is the assurance that God understands what I've gone through and will be going through because He knows my heart since He, too, experienced joys and pains in loving. It is still important to remember that if someone loves me, I have to love them back unconditionally because they are teaching me to love and open my heart and eyes to little things. Make every day count. Appreciate every moment and do everything that I possibly can, for I may never be able to experience it again. Falling out of love with the wrong guy is worth it because God has in store for me someone better or, shall I say, the best! He gave me my husband. I thank the Lord for giving me my better half, my loving, mature, responsible husband. Now, as I can forgive, move on, and move forward, I thank the Lord for all that has been. At times, my spirit needs to go through hard times to protect my soul. Going through pain makes me stronger, and having my heart broken makes me whole again. I know God will never leave me empty. He replaced what I had lost. He asked me to put something down because He wanted me to pick up something better. At times, I have to learn these things in a hard way. If given another chance, I will still choose to love again and again and again.

"Love 'til it hurts...it's worth it!"

Compassionate and loving God,

Thank you for the gift of LOVE. Thank you for the joys and pains of loving. My heart felt like it had been shattered, and my soul ached deeply from the wounds of love. In the depths of my pain, I struggled to understand Your ways, dear Lord. But through my tears and sorrow, I clung to Your promise. You had assured me that all things work together for the good of those who love You. Although I came to the point of questioning it, I still rely on You. You have never broken a promise to me. Thank you for giving me patience as I struggle. Thank you for making me stronger and bringing me closer to You...thank you for being my constant lover. Thank you for mending my broken heart and making me love again. My painful memories of loving were healed to a gift. God of love, as I learn to forgive myself, I humbly ask for Your grace to forgive those who have hurt me. I understand that, in one way or another, these pains and hurts have brought significant growth in my life. It was indeed beyond a blessing. Moreover, thank you for those who never tire of loving me. Thank you for my "Better Half," who gave his all to make me the woman I am now and who has been instrumental in making a better change in my life. Let me love him more and more each day, and let me truly realize from the depths of my being that when I love him, I have loved the God in me, and together, we will experience the happiness of one endless, immense love, and then we can really say we have truly loved our GOD!

Amen.

LOVING GOD COMPLETELY

"You shall love the Lord your God with all your heart, with all your soul, and will all your strength."

(Deuteronomy 6:5)

This verse from Deuteronomy 6:5 resonates deeply within me, lighting a path toward a meaningful and fulfilled life. When I think about what it means to love God wholeheartedly, I find inspiration to pour every part of myself into this relationship that transforms me from the inside out.

Loving God with all my heart is about embracing my emotions and desires, allowing them to intertwine with His will for my life. In this connection, I discover incredible joy and purpose, even in life's challenges. I have learned to see every moment—whether filled with laughter or tears—as an opportunity to grow closer to Him, to find His love in the midst of it all.

When I strive to love Him with all my soul, I seek deeper understanding and connection. This journey of faith becomes a quest for wisdom, clarity, and peace. In moments of prayer and reflection, I find solace and guidance, helping me navigate life's uncertainties with confidence. It is in these sacred moments that I truly feel alive as if my spirit is ignited by His presence.

Loving God with all my strength challenges me to channel my energy into meaningful actions. I realize that my love for Him is reflected in the way I treat others and serve my community. Whether it's through acts of kindness or lending a listening ear, I am inspired to let His love flow through me, making a difference in the lives of those around me. Each gesture, no matter how small, reminds me that I am part of something greater, a tapestry of love and connection.

Embracing this verse encourages me to live each day with intention and purpose. As I strive to love God fully, I am reminded that every action, every decision, and every relationship can harmonize with my faith. It gives me the strength to face adversity and the courage to pursue dreams that align with His vision for me.

Ultimately, this call to love God with my whole being inspires me to cultivate a life filled with gratitude, hope, and devotion. It is a journey of discovery, and with each step, I am reminded that my greatest fulfillment comes from embracing this divine love, allowing it to shape my path and illuminate my way. Each day becomes a new opportunity to reflect His light in the world, and for that, I am endlessly thankful.

Dear God,

As I reflect on Your presence in my life, I recognize You as the most faithful and loving being I could ever know. You are not just a friend; You are a perfect companion who stands by me during the highs and lows of life. I am profoundly grateful for Your unwavering support, especially in my moments of struggle and doubt. In my journey, I've often found my heart consumed by love for many—myself, my family, friends, and that special someone. However, I realize that in cherishing them, I sometimes overlook the depth of my love for You. It pains me to acknowledge that I have let other affections overshadow my relationship with You. Forgive me, Lord, for allowing my love for You to wane in comparison to my love for worldly things and people. Grant me the grace to teach my heart, to love You with all my being, to love You with all that I am—my heart, soul, and strength. Help me to emulate Your example of unconditional love, especially for those who are difficult to love. May I find true joy in loving the one true, faithful Lover of all—You.

Amen.

LOVING THE UNLOVABLE

"Love your neighbor as yourself. There is no commandment greater than these."

(Mark 12: 31)

Love is the very essence of who I am—it's what fuels my spirit and sustains me through life's ups and downs. I often think of love as my lifeblood, a vibrant force that empowers me to fully embrace the beauty in both giving and receiving. It feels as though I was truly born to love, to uncover and cultivate the deep connections that bring joy and richness to my life. Those relationships that resonate with my heart are the ones I treasure most; they fill my days with laughter, understanding, and a profound sense of belonging. Yet, this sentiment brings me to a profound realization—a deeper challenge that resides in extending my love to those who feel distant or difficult to connect with. In moments of comfort and ease, loving those who align with my values and beliefs feels natural and fulfilling. However, when I encounter individuals who challenge my views or who have caused me hurt, I feel a tug-of-war within myself. It's during these moments of discomfort that I am forced to confront the true essence of my character and what it means to love unconditionally. I have come to recognize that while my ability to love myself is crucial for my well-being, it can inadvertently create a barrier that limits my capacity to love others. This insight urges me to reflect on the very concept of loving my neighbor, which extends beyond my immediate circle and into the broader human experience. It encompasses every individual around me, including those who may have inflicted pain or disappointment in my life. It's a call to action that resonates deeply within me—a reminder that love should not be conditional or selective. The idea of loving my enemies and those who have hurt me can seem daunting. It's a challenging journey that requires me to dig deep into my own emotions and confront the conflicts that arise within. Yet, I have grown to believe that this path is essential for my spiritual growth and transformation. Embracing this challenge helps me expand my heart beyond its limits, fostering compassion and empathy that enriches my own soul. Each act of extended love—even when it feels uncomfortable—serves as a profound reminder of a calling greater than me. It teaches me invaluable lessons about humility, forgiveness, and the interconnectedness of all living beings. I begin to see that my ability to empathize with others, particularly those who seem undeserving of love, is not just an act of kindness—it's a significant step in my own spiritual journey. It allows me to break free from the confines of judgment and opens my heart to a universal truth: we all carry our own burdens, and love has the power to heal. Ultimately, this quest to love beyond my comfort zone feels like a divine invitation, a chance to grow into the truest version of myself. Embracing love in all its forms, even when it challenges me, illuminates my path toward deeper spiritual understanding. It reminds me that the essence of life is not solely found in joy and comfort but also in the courage to love those who test our hearts. Every act of compassion, every gesture of understanding, brings me closer to a profound realization—that love is the bridge that connects us all, guiding us toward unity and healing.

Dear God,

I come to You with a heart full of gratitude for the beautiful gift of love that surrounds my life in so many meaningful ways. Each day, I am reminded of how blessed I am to have people in my life who show me what love truly means, each in their own unique way. Thank You for the relationships I cherish, for the laughter shared, the tears shed, and the joyful moments that connect us. These experiences enrich my life and teach me the true depth of connection that Your presence brings.

I look to Your Son, Jesus, as the ultimate example of selfless love. His life shines as a beacon, guiding the path I strive to follow. His willingness to sacrifice for others, to forgive, and to embrace those who feel lost inspires me every day. I aspire to reflect that kind of love in my own life, to become a living testament to His teachings. May my actions reflect Your love, even when faced with challenges or indifference, for I know that true love requires perseverance and dedication.

Help me cultivate a heart that is forgiving and open. In a world where judgment often takes precedence over understanding, guide me to reach out to those who may seem unlovable or distant. Remind me that everyone deserves compassion and that even the hardest hearts can be softened by a simple act of kindness. Teach me to see You in every person I encounter, to recognize the value in each soul, and to extend my hand and heart without reservation.

As I go through my daily interactions, let me be aware of the chance to bring Your light into the lives of others. Help me view every moment as an opportunity to act with love and to shine brightly in the darker corners of the world. Whether it's sharing a smile with a stranger, lending a listening ear to a friend in need, or offering encouragement to someone feeling defeated, may I be diligent in spreading love and kindness like seeds in good soil.

When I love deeply, let it reflect my love for You. May my heart mirror the boundless, unconditional love You have shown me. Allow my words and actions to testify to Your grace and glory, shining brightly for all to see. Help me to be a source of peace, a voice for the voiceless, and a source of joy for those who are weary.

Thank You for Your endless grace and for the love that transforms my heart each day. Every breath I take reminds me of love's incredible power—its ability to heal, uplift, and create connections that break down barriers. May I never take this gift for granted but embrace it fully, allowing it to shape who I am and define my purpose.

As I continue on my journey, may I always find ways to love others as You love me. Help me remember that love is not just a feeling but an action, a commitment to serve, give, and cherish. I lay all these prayers before You, trusting in Your guidance and grace.

Amen.

MY RING AND HIS GRACE

Then he adds: "Their sins and lawless acts I will remember no more."

(Hebrews 10:17)

One Sunday, on Mother's Day at church, I sat quietly in the pew, reflecting on the love and sacrifices of mothers around the world. As I clasped my hands in worship, I noticed something that sank my heart. One of the diamond stones from my engagement ring was missing. Panic washed over me as I tried to recall if I had hit my hand against something earlier. I couldn't remember, but I knew the precious stone was gone, and I had no idea where it could be.

I dreaded the moment I would have to tell my husband about my carelessness. The thought of his possible disappointment weighed heavily on my heart. How would he react? Would he be upset? Would he think I was irresponsible? These questions swirled in my mind, adding to my anxiety. But when I finally mustered the courage to tell him, his response was extraordinary. He showed great compassion and care as if to silently assure me that it was just a ring and that everything would be okay.

Every time I remember the missing stone, I can't help but feel the urge to earn his grace. Yet, he never holds this incident against me. Instead, he took the ring to the jeweler and had it fixed.

This experience made me reflect on my relationship with God and my understanding of His grace. Too often, I think of my sins and feel like I must do something to earn God's forgiveness. I replay my mistakes and shortcomings, feeling unworthy of His love. But then I'm reminded of His promise in Hebrews 10:17: "Their sins and lawless acts I will remember no more." God, in His infinite mercy, forgives and forgets our transgressions. He doesn't hold grudges or keep a record of our wrongs. This truth brings a profound sense of relief and comfort, knowing that His grace is freely given, not something I can earn.

In moments of weakness, when my faith wavers and I feel burdened by guilt and shame, I turn to God's Word for comfort. I remember that His grace is a gift freely given through faith in Jesus Christ. I can do nothing to earn it; it stands as a testament to His boundless love and mercy. This knowledge reassures me that despite my imperfections, He loves me unconditionally and offers forgiveness.

As I walk through the ebbs and flows of life, I hold onto this truth. God's grace is sufficient for me, and His power is made perfect in my weakness. His love covers all my sins and washes away my guilt. In these moments, I find peace and strength in knowing that He understands my struggles and walks with me every step of the way.

When I think of my husband's response to the missing diamond, I see a reflection of God's grace in our relationship. Just as my husband showed me compassion and love, God extends His grace to me, even when I feel undeserving. It's a beautiful reminder that His love is steadfast and unwavering.

Dear God,

I come before You with a humble heart, grateful for Your endless love and grace that surrounds me. Thank You for the countless blessings in my life, especially for the relationships that mirror Your compassion and understanding. Your presence in my life is a constant source of strength, and I am forever grateful for Your guidance.

As I reflect on my imperfections and the times I have felt unworthy, I ask for Your forgiveness and strength. Help me remember that Your grace is sufficient and that I do not have to earn Your love. Teach me to trust in Your promise that You remember my sins no more and to find comfort and reassurance in Your Word.

In moments of weakness and doubt, remind me of Your unwavering presence beside me. Grant me the courage to embrace Your forgiveness and to extend that same grace to others. Teach me to let go of guilt and shame, replacing it with peace and joy in Your unconditional love. Your mercy is boundless, and I am thankful for the opportunity to start anew each day with a heart full of Your love.

Thank you for the people You place in my life, like my husband, who exemplify kindness and support. His love and compassion reflect Your grace, and I am grateful for his presence in my life. Help me cherish these relationships and offer the same compassion that You've shown me. May I be a source of support and encouragement to others, just as You have been to me.

As I walk through the trials of life, fill my heart with faith, knowing that Your power is made perfect in my weakness. When I feel overwhelmed, remind me that Your strength is always available and that I can rely on Your guidance. Help me find joy in the small moments and appreciate the beauty in each day. May I find strength in Your love and carry it with me in all I do.

Thank You for Your endless grace and forgiveness. Help me to live a life that reflects Your love and to always turn to You in times of need. I am grateful for Your presence in my life and the ways You continue to shape and guide me.

Amen.

OBEDIENCE

"If you love me, keep my commands" (John 14:15)

I realize how deeply rooted the concept of obedience is in my life. Growing up in the Philippines, my parents instilled in my siblings and me a strong sense of duty to listen to and respect our elders. This idea of obedience became even more pronounced when I entered religious life years ago, where we learned to follow our formators closely. However, as I've matured and gained more life experience, I've come to realize that obedience isn't always straightforward. It can be a struggle, especially when my own values clash with what I'm being asked to do. There have been moments when I followed orders without really understanding or agreeing with them, simply out of habit or expectation. Stepping outside of what feels comfortable to obey has often been a tough journey for me. It sometimes feels like that process of being shaped and molded, akin to a rough stone becoming something beautiful. There are times, too when I find myself looking for an easy escape. When things feel too complex or daunting, my instinct is to resist. As a Christian, I get that loving God means obeying His commands. But let's be honest, that's often easier said than done. Following the path that Jesus walked, especially knowing the sacrifice He made, requires a lot from me. Still, I know deep down that this path offers a fulfillment that is worth striving for. In my spiritual journey, I'm learning that obedience isn't just about following rules; it's about trusting God's plan and surrendering my own desires. It's finding meaning in those uncomfortable moments, realizing that they often lead to growth. Just like a potter works with clay, God uses those challenging times to mold us into who we're meant to be. When I think about Jesus' obedience, even when faced with the ultimate sacrifice on the cross, it moves me deeply. His dedication to God's will, regardless of the suffering He endured, motivates me to trust and follow. It's a powerful reminder that obeying God is also an expression of love and trust, knowing He's with me through it all. As I move forward, I find myself praying for strength against my own resistance and for the wisdom to recognize what God wants from me. I believe that through obedience, I'll discover a deeper connection with Him and that He'll guide me through every challenge. I strive to reflect Christ's example, understanding that true fulfillment comes from aligning my life with His purpose. I ask for God's grace to help me live out His commands with genuine faith and courage. I want to be open to the lessons He teaches me through obedience, ready to follow His path, even when it feels tough. This reflection captures not just the struggles I have with obedience but also my commitment to trusting in God's plan. It's a heartfelt expression of the challenges and rewards that come with a life of faith and dedication.

Dear God,

I come to You with a humble heart, recognizing how important obedience is in my life. With gratitude, I look back on the journey You've guided me through—every moment full of lessons and insights that have shaped who I am today. Thank You for the grace You've shown me, especially in those uncertain times when the path ahead was unclear. Your presence has always been a source of strength and comfort, and for that, I am truly grateful.

While I journey through the intricacies of life, I sincerely ask for Your help in fully embracing Your will. Sometimes, I feel overwhelmed by the decisions I face and the choices before me. Please give me the faith to trust in Your plans, even when the way is not clear or when challenges seem too great. Help me to see the beauty in the journey of obedience, even when it involves sacrifice or patience.

Lord, I ask for the strength to follow Your teachings with unwavering commitment. I want to live according to Your Word, embodying the values and principles You've placed in my heart. May I find joy in serving You, knowing that my actions can contribute to a greater purpose.

Help me to always seek what is pleasing in Your sight, finding fulfillment in the small acts of kindness that align with Your vision for humanity.

Teach me to surrender my will to Yours. Letting go of my desires and expectations is often tough, but I know that doing so can lead to a deeper sense of peace and direction. I pray that You guide my heart and mind, helping me to be mindful of my choices each day so that I can align myself more closely with Your divine purpose.

Grant me the wisdom and discernment to hear Your voice amidst the noise and distractions of everyday life. I often seek direction in various ways, but I want to hear Your guidance clearly. Surround me with Your love, filling my heart with the peace that only You can provide. I hope to reflect Your light in the world, shining brightly for others to find hope.

Help me remember that obedience to You is more than just following rules; it's about trusting in Your greater plan and surrendering my desires. It's recognizing that every command and teaching comes from Your compassion and love for me. May I experience Your endless love in ways that inspire me to share that love with everyone I meet.

I want to show kindness and grace to others, reminding them of their worth and the infinite love present in this world. I pray to be a source of encouragement and support, sharing the light You've given me. Let my actions reflect the belief that everyone deserves compassion, understanding, and kindness, no matter their circumstances. Thank You for Your boundless love and compassion. May my life be a testament to Your goodness, showing everyone that obedience is not just a duty but a privilege—a chance to walk closely with You and to take part in Your plans on earth.

Amen.

Painter's Tape

"If we confess our sins, he is faithful and just and will forgive us our sins and purify us from all unrighteousness."

(1 John 1:9)

I find a strange sense of peace in house projects and cleaning. There's something incredibly therapeutic about bringing order to chaos. However, the challenge arises when the house refuses to stay clean—especially with a lively child around. It's hard not to feel frustrated when everything gets messy just moments after I've tidied up.

One day, my husband and I were painting our living room. We were prepping with painter's tape, and my husband remarked, "I am so glad this tape is forgiving." His words hit me hard. I wished I could be as forgiving as that tape. I often find myself getting worked up over tiny irritations, making it tough to let go and move forward.

I've come to understand that much of my frustration arises from a desire for control and perfection. When things don't go according to plan, it's easy to let irritation take hold. But I've realized that clinging to anger only harms me and those I care about. It creates a cloud over my judgment and puts strain on my relationships.

But then I'm reminded of God's grace. As 1 John 1:9 says, if we confess our sins, He is faithful and just to forgive us and cleanse us from all unrighteousness. God's forgiveness is perfect, and it's a model for how I should strive to live—patiently, lovingly, and with a heart willing to forgive.

Life with a child is messy, and that's okay. It's a part of the journey. What's important is how I respond. I need to extend grace and patience, not just to my loved ones but to myself as well. Just as I strive to tidy and organize my home, I must also seek to cleanse my spirit through God's forgiveness and share that same grace with others.

Through God's grace, I can find the strength to let go of my frustrations and embrace the beauty of forgiveness. It's not about maintaining a spotless home; it's about cultivating a heart overflowing with love and grace. I'm discovering how to forgive my child for the spills, let go of the little things my husband does that frustrate me, and, most importantly, forgive myself for my imperfections.

Forgiveness doesn't equate to ignoring the mess or the mistakes. It means acknowledging them, addressing the issues, and then moving forward—much like how God handles our missteps. This is a continuous journey that demands daily effort and prayer.

As I strive to embody God's grace, I find the heaviness of anger releasing its grip on me, replaced by a deep sense of peace and love. This journey isn't always easy, but with God walking alongside me, I'm learning to live life with a forgiving heart.

Dear God,

Today, I come to You seeking peace and understanding in my daily life. Please grant me the patience to face the challenges ahead, especially when the weight of responsibility feels overwhelming.

Help me to extend forgiveness to those around me—my child, my spouse, and myself. Teach me how to release anger and frustration, filling that void with Your love and grace. May my interactions reflect Your forgiving nature, allowing me to be patient and kind in all that I do.

Remind me that true peace arises from a heart filled with Your spirit. Guide me in cleansing my heart and mind with Your mercy, lifting the burden of anger and replacing it with everlasting peace. Help me embrace the beauty of forgiveness and live a life rich in love and grace.

As I journey through life, may I find strength in Your presence, knowing that with Your guidance, I can overcome my struggles and find joy in the everyday moments. Let Your grace illuminate my path, leading me to a life of peace, love, and forgiveness.

Amen.

PATIENCE

"Be joyful in hope, patient in affliction, faithful in prayer."

(Romans 12:12)

Patience is certainly a virtue, but if I'm being honest, it's been a lifelong struggle for me. I find that I often get disappointed easily when things don't go the way I expect or when situations unfold beyond my control. It's like I have this inner clock that starts ticking faster, and when the time runs out, my frustration bubbles up. Whether it's waiting for a friend to show up or dealing with a long line at the grocery store, I feel this impatience creeping in.

When it comes to people, I really struggle with those who are insensitive or hard to understand. It's tough for me to empathize when I feel like they're not meeting me halfway. I think part of my issue is that I hold high standards—not just for myself but for others, too. And when someone doesn't meet those standards, I find myself growing impatient and annoyed. I recognize that this can come off as prideful, and deep down, I know it's an area I need to work on.

The practice of patience often feels daunting because it requires me to look beyond my own desires and fears. I've realized that my selfishness plays a big role in my struggle. I often prioritize my own feelings and timelines, and that makes it hard for me to be patient with others. Plus, there's this fear of vulnerability that comes with being patient; it's like I'm afraid to let go of my instant gratification and the comfort of being in control.

Still, I understand that cultivating patience could lead to a greater capacity for love—both for Christ and for my neighbors. There's a part of me that craves that deeper connection, and I know that practicing patience could be a stepping stone toward that. It's just a challenge to remind myself of that during those moments when my frustration flares up.

I often find myself reflecting on how I can change my perspective. Maybe it's about embracing the messiness of life and realizing that everyone has their own struggles. As I keep working on this, I hope to find ways to be more patient, more understanding, and ultimately, more loving toward myself and those around me. It's a journey, but I know it's one that can lead to a richer life filled with deeper relationships and a more profound sense of peace.

Dear God,

As I come before You with a humble heart, I want to reflect deeply on the importance of obedience in my life. I see how vital it is to align my actions with Your will, and I'm grateful for the guidance You've offered throughout my journey. Every step I've taken has been illuminated by Your light, teaching me valuable lessons and providing insights that have shaped my character and my faith in profound ways.

With every challenge I've encountered, I've witnessed how Your grace has been my steadfast companion, especially during times of uncertainty when the path ahead felt clouded. I thank You for Your unwavering support, even in moments when I struggled to trust in the process. There have been times when I felt lost and overwhelmed by life's burdens and the expectations I placed on myself. Yet during those moments, Your presence was a sanctuary of strength, reminding me that I am never truly alone. For Your constant love and guidance, I am truly thankful.

As I sit here now, I approach You with a heart eager to grow in patience. I know I have my own struggles and shortcomings—traits that sometimes hinder my relationships and personal growth. In these moments of reflection, I'm reminded of Your enduring grace, which is the foundation of my spiritual journey.

I aspire to embody patience, yet I understand it goes beyond just waiting. It's about responding to others with love, understanding, and compassion—even when it's difficult. Help me to remember that everyone I encounter is fighting their own battles, often hidden from view. In a world where everyone carries their own burdens, guide me to be more compassionate and empathetic.

Thank You for Your incredible patience with me and for the countless lessons I continue to learn. Each day brings an opportunity for growth, and I surrender my impatience to You, trusting that with Your gentle guidance, I can become a more loving and patient person. May Your grace empower me to extend to others the understanding that I seek for myself.

When impatience creeps in and frustration rises, remind me to pause and take a deep breath. Help me to see beyond my immediate feelings and understand the circumstances surrounding others. I want to let go of my pride and the unrealistic standards I often impose on myself and those around me. It's important to appreciate that everyone is on their own unique journey and to recognize the beauty that can come from waiting. In doing so, I hope to build deeper connections and foster a greater love for those in my life.

May I come to understand that patience is an act of love and a form of respect for Your divine timing. Lord, I earnestly ask for Your wisdom to nurture a heart that listens well and remains slow to frustration. Fill me with Your spirit so that I can embody the love of Christ in all aspects of my life. Help me approach every interaction with kindness and understanding, viewing each moment as an opportunity to reflect Your love.

Thank You for Your incredible patience with me and for the countless lessons I continue to learn. Each day brings an opportunity for growth, and I surrender my impatience to You, trusting that with Your gentle guidance, I can become a more loving and patient person. May Your grace empower me to extend to others the understanding that I seek for myself.

As I strive for these goals, I seek peace in knowing that Your timing is perfect. Help me to find solace in moments of waiting, recognizing that they often lead to growth and transformation. On this journey, I look forward to becoming not just a better individual but a more faithful servant in Your kingdom.

Amen.

SHAPED FOR DIVINE SERVICE

"There are different kinds of working, but in all of them and in everyone it is the same God at work."

(1 Corinthians 12:6)

I often think about the journey each of us takes in life and how we're all connected in this big world. The verse from 1 Corinthians 12:6 reminds me that even though our paths are different, we're all guided by the same force.

I believe I am more than just a collection of experiences. I see myself as a unique creation designed with purpose. Life can feel like a rollercoaster with its ups and downs, but as I look back, I realize that every moment—good or bad—has shaped who I am. Each experience is like a brushstroke on the canvas of my life, contributing to the bigger picture of who I am.

From the moment I was born, I believe God had a plan for me. This idea brings me comfort. Every joy I've had, every challenge I've faced, and even the small, everyday moments have all contributed to my growth. When I think about the lessons I've learned, the people I've met, and the obstacles I've overcome, I can see how they've all helped shape my character. Each challenge has taught me important lessons in resilience and patience, while my happy moments have taught me to be grateful.

During times when I doubt myself, I remind myself that I'm not alone on this journey. It brings me peace knowing I am supported. Each new day is a chance to grow, to lend a hand, and to share kindness with others. I've learned that my experiences allow me to connect with people in meaningful ways. Whether I'm understanding someone's struggles or celebrating their good times, those connections matter.

As I continue on this path, I accept that I am a work in progress. Each day comes with its own challenges and chances to grow. I've learned to embrace this journey, even when it feels uncertain. There is beauty in the process of learning from life's twists and turns. I am thankful for how God has shaped me for a purpose.

Believing in this larger plan helps me value even the smallest moments. It's in little things, like a friendly smile from a stranger or a laugh with a friend, that I see how everything connects. I truly believe every experience has meaning and contributes to the bigger picture.

As I look ahead, I feel hopeful about what's to come. Each day is part of my unique story, but it's also part of the larger human experience. Embracing this journey helps me live with purpose and appreciate both the highs and lows, knowing that everything is shaping me into who I'm meant to be.

Dear God,

I come before You with a grateful heart, reflecting on the unique journey You've placed before me. Thank You for reminding me that while our paths may differ, we are all connected through Your divine presence. I find strength in the truth of 1 Corinthians 12:6.

Help me to recognize that I am more than just my experiences; I am a creation designed with purpose. Thank You for shaping me through each moment of joy and challenge I have faced. I appreciate how every experience, big or small, has contributed to who I am becoming. May I learn to embrace the lessons from life's ups and downs and see them as brushstrokes on the canvas of my life.

In times of doubt, remind me that I am never alone. Please guide me daily as I strive to grow, serve, and share kindness with those around me. Help me connect with others more deeply, understanding their struggles and celebrating their joys. Let my life be a vessel of Your love and grace.

As I continue this journey, help me accept that I am a work in progress. Grant me the wisdom to appreciate each day and recognize the beauty in each experience, even the little ones. I trust in Your plan for my life and believe every moment shapes me for a purpose.

Thank You for the hope that fills my heart as I look ahead. Help me to live with intention and find joy in both the highs and the lows. Guide me as I walk this path, knowing I am becoming who You created me to be.

Amen.

SWEET FRIENDSHIP

"Perfume and incense bring joy to the heart, and the pleasantness of a friend springs from their heartfelt advice."

(Proverbs 27:9)

The special bond between my best friend, Mariton, and I began back in high school, but our story started even earlier, back in preschool. Over the years, our friendship has blossomed from childhood playmates into lifelong companions. This connection has been an endless source of joy and support for both of us.

Mariton and I have experienced countless moments together—laughter, tears, and all the ups and downs life throws our way. We've cheered each other on in good times and comforted each other in harder times, sharing our deepest fears, wildest dreams, and profound sorrows. Our friendship isn't just about celebrating the happy moments; it's about standing together when life gets tough.

One of the most touching things about our friendship is how much Mariton cares for my family. Whenever she visits our home country, she always makes it a point to stop by and give my mom a warm hug and a kiss from me. That simple act shows just how deep our friendship runs.

Even though we're 2,000 miles apart, our bond remains unbreakable. We may not see each other as often as we'd like, but we stay connected through phone calls, messages, and the occasional visit. Each time we reunite is a precious opportunity to reconnect and create more memories together.

I often think about how beautifully our friendship reflects certain stories from the Bible. The bond between David and Jonathan reminds me of the loyalty we share, while Jesus' friendship with Lazarus demonstrates a profound connection. Jesus wept when Lazarus died, showcasing the pain that can come with losing a dear friend. These stories resonate with our experiences, highlighting the importance of loyalty, love, and support in true friendship.

Good friends are a rare treasure. They stand by us through thick and thin, drawing us closer to God, especially when the challenges of life threaten to pull us apart. True friendship mirrors the love of Jesus, who promises, "And surely I am with you always, to the very end of the age." (Matthew 28:20)

In times of doubt, Mariton has been my rock, guiding me back to faith and reminding me of God's unwavering love. Her thoughtful advice and prayers have comforted me and provided strength during life's stormy seas.

In a world that often feels chaotic, the constancy of a true friend brings so much comfort and joy. Although Mariton and I are separated by distance, our bond remains as strong as ever. Our friendship is a testament to the power of love, loyalty, and faith. It reminds us that no matter where we are in the world, we are never alone because we have each other and God's unfailing love.

Dear God,

Thank you for the gift of friendship. Your Word tells us that "a friend loves at all times" (Proverbs 17:17), and we are truly blessed by the friends you've brought into our lives.

Lord Jesus, you've shown us the true meaning of friendship through your life. You loved deeply and sacrificially, reminding us that "greater love has no one than this: to lay down one's life for one's friends" (John 15:13). May we follow your example and be true friends to those around us.

Heavenly Father, bless our friendships. Help us be loyal, supportive, and understanding, just as you are. Grant us the wisdom to give heartfelt advice and the compassion to be present in times of need. May our friendships be a source of joy, comfort, and strength, bringing us closer to you and each other.

We also pray for those who may feel lonely or disconnected. Surround them with loving friends who will uplift and encourage them. Let your presence be a constant source of comfort and companionship in their lives.

Help us to be friends who reflect your love and grace. When our friends face trials, may we support and encourage them. When they succeed, may we celebrate with genuine happiness. Let our friendships be a testament to your love and faithfulness.

We pray for the strength to forgive and seek reconciliation when misunderstandings arise. Help us extend the same grace and mercy you've shown us. May we always strive to build each other up with words of life and encouragement.

Finally, we lift our friends who are struggling with doubts in their faith. Use us as instruments of your love to guide them back to you, reminding them of your promises and the hope we find in Christ. May our friendships lead to spiritual growth, drawing us closer to you.

Thank you, Jesus, for being our perfect and faithful friend. Your promise to be with us always brings peace and reassurance. May we reflect your love in our relationships every day.

Amen.

THE HEART OF CREATION

"26 Then God said, "Let us make mankind in our image, in our likeness, so that they may rule over the fish in the sea and the birds in the sky, over the livestock and all the wild animals, and over all the creatures that move along the ground." 27 So God created mankind in his own image, in the image of God he created them; male and female he created them.28 God blessed them and said to them, "Be fruitful and increase in number; fill the earth and subdue it. Rule over the fish in the sea and the birds in the sky and over every living creature that moves on the ground." 29 Then God said, "I give you every seed-bearing plant on the face of the whole earth and every tree that has fruit with seed in it. They will be yours for food. 30 And to all the beasts of the earth and all the birds in the sky and all the creatures that move along the ground—everything that has the breath of life in it—I give every green plant for food." And it was so.31 God saw all that he had made, and it was very good. And there was evening, and there was morning—the sixth day.

(Genesis 1: 26-31)

Reflecting on my younger years, I often wondered if I truly mattered to God. The Creation Account in Genesis provided the answer. From its very first words, it's clear that God had me in mind. Before I even entered this world, God's plan included ME. My loving parents took special care to prepare for my arrival, ensuring everything was ready and in place for me to thrive. God exemplifies this kind of caring preparation, and the Genesis Creation Account illustrates everything God did to make my existence possible. He wanted a perfect place for me—and for everyone.

My loving parents took special care of me before I was born. They made sure everything was ready, everything was in place, and everything I needed to grow as their precious child was available. God is indeed the exemplary model of this caring and perfect preparation. The Creation Account in the book of Genesis depicts all that God did to prepare for me. God desired a perfect place for me and everybody.

The Genesis account showcases the careful attention God put into creating everything with a purpose. That purpose includes you, me, and everyone. On the sixth day, God created man in His image because He wanted to connect with us, to form a loving relationship where He could shower us with love and receive our love in return. The Creation Account is fundamentally about LOVE—God's profound love for all of us. This love focuses on our needs, ensuring that every part of creation supports our ability to succeed and flourish. God entrusted us with authority over all creation, all out of love.

As I grew older and became more aware of the world around me, I couldn't help but notice the damaging consequences of humanity's actions on the natural environment. It pains me to witness the heartless destruction that has arisen from our neglect and abuse of God's creation. This abuse threatens not just our environment but also the very fabric of life itself.

Mankind has been given the honor of stewardship, tasked with having dominion over the earth (Genesis 1:28). Yet, we have strayed from this sacred role, often treating the earth as if we owned it rather than nurturing it with love and respect.

Unfortunately, in our era of self-centeredness, we seem to have lost sight of the sacredness of creation, treating it with a cruelty that cannot last indefinitely. The earth itself groans under the weight of our neglect, crying out for change. If we continue down this path, the consequences will ultimately lead to our own downfall. I sincerely hope that humanity will recognize the value of this precious gift—the creation—and cultivate a sense of gratitude. We must pray for its well-being and do our part to safeguard the environment. It is imperative that each of us respects the natural world and that those in positions of power act decisively to ensure its conservation and protection.

Dear God,

I come to You with an open heart, eager to connect and find Your presence. Life gets so busy, and sometimes, I forget to take a moment to appreciate the beauty around me. Help me pause and truly see the wonder of creation—in the gentle songs of birds at dawn and the breathtaking flashes of lightning at night. You are everywhere in nature, showing Yourself in its calmness and power, and I'm always in awe of Your work.

I'm grateful for the still waters that reflect the vibrant colors of the world and the peaceful landscapes that bring serenity to my soul. I realize that in my quest for growth and success, I've sometimes taken more than I needed, hurting the precious gifts You've given us. I acknowledge my mistakes and ask for forgiveness for any harm I've caused to Your beautiful world.

Help me to slow down and truly appreciate the gifts and blessings You've generously shared with me. Teach me to find joy in the simple moments and to see the abundance of Your love in everything around me. Guide my choices and actions so they align with Your plans for me.

Grant me the strength to care for Your creation, treating it with the respect and love it deserves. Help me be a responsible steward of the earth so that the legacy I leave behind reflects care, compassion, and reverence for all that You have created.

In my daily life, may I always be aware of the impact I have on the environment and those around me. Fill me with Your spirit so that I can share Your love and patience in all I do. Let my actions show my gratitude for the wonders of creation and my commitment to preserving it for future generations.

Thank You for the beauty and majesty of the world You've made. I surrender my faults and impatience to You, trusting that with Your support, I can grow into a more loving, patient, and responsible person. May my life reflect Your work in me and bring glory to Your name.

Amen.

Unfailing Love
(A Tribute To All Mothers In the World)

"As a mother comforts her child,
so will I comfort you..."

(Isaiah 66:13)

My brothers and I called her Mama. We all knew a wonderful story about her since we were young.

This story unfolded in a hospital in 1984 when my brother Cannon was just eight months old and was diagnosed with a life-threatening intestinal condition. As a young child, I witnessed firsthand the emotional turmoil and unwavering faith of my family during this crisis. My mother's heart was shattered as she watched her infant son suffer. She sought solace in prayer and the support of loved ones, desperately pleading for a miracle. The doctors presented a grim prognosis: a risky surgery with a limited lifespan or a painful waiting game. Mama chose hope, clinging to faith for a miracle. She was praying with a desperation I'd never seen in her before, pleading with God to spare her son by offering her own life in exchange.

Then, suddenly, my brother's heartbeat ceased. "He's dead!" declared the doctor. Amidst the shock, I heard Mama's vehement protest, "Do not touch my baby; he is alive!" She resisted the doctors' attempts to detach the tubes, even as evidence suggested all hope was lost. Yet, the prayer group's faith did not waver, their prayers filling the tense silence. After what felt like an eternity, marked by fifteen minutes of profound grief, an unexpected sign of life emerged—my brother miraculously showed signs of recovery, astonishing everyone, including the medical staff. It was a moment of undeniable proof that a mother's prayers were heard.

A mother's love is the purest, most enduring bond, surpassing all other forms of relationship, proven through time and trials. My mother embodies divine love on earth, sharing in my pain, comforting me in her embrace, and being my pillar of strength when I falter. Her sacrifices and love are beyond repayment; her actions and presence a constant source of special meaning in my life. She is my most cherished treasure, understanding me deeply and offering unwavering support. Her love is the essence of my being, and her example of unconditional love is a legacy that will endure forever, teaching me the true depth of a mother's love. This love mirrors that of OUR BLESSED MOTHER MARY at the cross—unfailing, courageous, and profound, sharing in every pain and loss. The depth of a mother's love is immeasurable. Mama's love is boundless and magnificent, a source of strength in my life. She is irreplaceable.

I dedicate this story to all mothers around the world whose love and sacrifice are truly invaluable.

And to my dear Mama...my love for you is eternal.

From a daughter's heart...

Dear God,

I come to you with a heart full of gratitude for all the mothers in the world, those incredible women to whom You have entrusted the sacred responsibility of nurturing and caring for every precious life from its very beginning. Each mother carries a unique story, a journey that shapes not only their own lives but also the lives of their children. In a particularly special way, I want to thank You for the gift of my Mama. She is not just a mother to me; she is an integral part of who I am. From my earliest memories, she has been my steadfast pillar, always offering me love and support in ways that words often fail to express. Her gentle hands have shaped my character, her wise words have guided my decisions, and her unwavering faith in me has given me the strength to pursue my dreams. No one else in this world has the same understanding of me, the same ability to see my potential even when I'm filled with doubt. She is my best friend—someone with whom I can share my joys and sorrows without fear of judgment. I find comfort in her presence, and I cherish the countless moments we share, whether it's through deep conversations or simple laughter over everyday life. I recognize that she is not perfect, and that is part of what makes her so extraordinary. She has her struggles and insecurities, yet she faces each day with a bravery that inspires me. In my eyes, she comes remarkably close to perfection, for her heart is filled with kindness and her actions are rooted in love. As I reflect on her sacrifices and the life lessons she has imparted, I pray for her protection and well-being. Please bless her with good health and happiness, and let her feel the immense love that surrounds her. I also ask for Your blessings upon all mothers around the world. May they find inspiration and strength in their daily lives, and may they feel appreciated for the incredible work they do, often unnoticed. Please grant that they may mirror the qualities of our Blessed Mother—her humility, her unwavering fidelity, and her self-giving love. Help all mothers to nurture their children with the same grace and devotion, lighting their paths with wisdom and compassion. Thank you, Almighty Father, for the remarkable gift of motherhood.

Amen.

Vigilant Heart

I've come to a profound realization that my life often feels like it's merely dragging along because I'm not truly living it. Instead, I find myself constantly waiting for "tomorrow," with the hope that it will bring something "beautiful." While it's true that there is indeed a "beautiful tomorrow" ahead, it usually doesn't align with my expectations.

I tend to look forward to vacations or special moments, but once they're over, I'm left with a sense of dissatisfaction. This feeling of incompleteness triggers a cycle where I begin to seek out the next thing to anticipate. The reality, however, is that there's an unavoidable aspect of life—the inevitable meeting with the Lord who is to come. This is the "beautiful tomorrow" that I subconsciously yearn for. I was created for happiness, and only He can provide me with that true joy.

Since I don't know when Christ will return—be it today, tonight, or in a year—I must remain vigilant, much like those who keep watch because they don't know when the thief will arrive. Like many others, I may fear death and try to push it out of my mind, yet it remains an inevitable part of life. Jesus himself experienced it, reminding us that earthly life is fleeting, but that doesn't diminish its value. In fact, every moment we experience is precious, and we must strive to live it to its fullest, preparing ourselves for our final encounter with Him.

The passage, *"But about that day or hour no one knows, not even the angels in heaven, nor the Son, but only the Father but only the Father"* (Matthew 24:36), resonates deeply with me. It brings back memories of my elementary days at St. Mary Mazzarello School, Philippines. Back in 6th grade, we had a particularly intimidating teacher who could effortlessly discern who had studied and who had not. I recall the anxiety of being picked to recite in front of the class. Those who were unprepared would be humiliated, left scratching their heads in embarrassment. I often pretended to know the answers, but inside, I was terrified.

Eventually, though, we all raised our hands because we had worked hard to learn the material. Despite my fears, this experience taught me the importance of being prepared. Likewise, I want to be ready on my final day—not hiding in fear but confident in my relationship with Him. I aim to stand confidently, raising my hand, eager to respond. I want to be able to say, "He loved me. He died for me! And even though I'm imperfect, I've tried to follow Him." I can only be ready for that moment if I've spent my life preparing for it.

Dear God,

In the quiet of this moment, I come before You with an open heart. I recognize that too often, I am caught in a cycle of waiting for tomorrow, longing for moments of beauty without fully embracing the present. Help me to find joy in each day, to see the value in the ordinary, and to trust that every moment holds significance in Your plan. As I reflect on the truth of Your return, I am reminded of the importance of being prepared. Grant me the strength and courage to live my life in a way that honors You. Teach me to raise my hand confidently, not in fear, but in love and gratitude for the sacrifice You made for me. May I strive to deepen my relationship with You every day so that when I stand before You, I do so with a heart full of faith and love. Help me to embrace life fully, cherishing both the joys and the challenges, knowing that each moment brings me closer to You. Let me be vigilant and ready, living a life marked by purpose and devotion, so that I may one day hear Your invitation to eternal joy. Thank You for Your unwavering love and for the beautiful tomorrow that awaits me in Your presence. Guide me as I seek to live in the light of that promise.

Amen.

www.ingramcontent.com/pod-product-compliance
Lightning Source LLC
Chambersburg PA
CBHW051210120626
46547CB00013B/1282